How to Lead the Church

A Practical Guide to Growing Healthy Congregations

SECOND INTERNATIONAL EDITION

Dale Hummel
***with* David Aeilts**

Wooddale Church
Eden Prairie, Minnesota, U.S.

Editor: Grace Smith

Illustrators: Kayla Harren, kaylaharren@gmail.com; Dan Volenec, dan@danvolenec.com

Publisher: Wooddale Worldwide, 6630 Shady Oak Road, Eden Prairie, Minnesota 55344, U.S.
www.wooddale.org

ISBN 978-0-9980768-3-6

Library of Congress Control Number: 2019910891

Second International Edition

DEDICATION

To my wife, Marcia, who has sacrificed my being away many weeks of the year. She is a true partner in ministry.

To my missionary parents, Jim and Virginia Hummel, who modeled for me a love for other cultures.

To the leaders and congregations of The Compass Church and Wooddale Church, who encouraged and supported me in bringing the hope of the Gospel here, near and far.

To Stephen Chandra, who invited and challenged me to discover God at work in Asia.

To Richard Payne, Global Missions Pastor of Wooddale Church, who inspired the vision to put my teachings in this book.

TABLE OF CONTENTS

FOREWORD

Clear and Simple

So easy to understand, and yet SOLID!

Dale Hummel's *How to Lead the Church* is just like his teaching, biblically balanced to the core! When Dale teaches, the Scriptures come alive! It is even so with this book.

Pauls and Timothys, you are going to love *How to Lead the Church* as much as you have loved his messages. You will be engaged, hanging onto every word.

You will listen. You will laugh. You will learn. Whether Dale discusses leadership in the church or leadership of self, character, or competency, you will be challenged to become men and women of God who will impact your nation for the kingdom!

The Timothy Initiative (TTI) has no greater friend than Dale Hummel. He writes from his heart, with one desire only: to help us be the disciple-makers God has called us to be. So read the book. Enjoy it. Then do what it says. Lead!

May God grant us an earth-shaking movement of disciple-makers everywhere, until the whole world knows!

David Nelms
Founder and President
The Timothy Initiative

INTRODUCTION

Leading Is Like Farming

My grandfather was a farmer. He learned from his father the skills necessary to prepare the soil, plant the seed, and raise crops that would produce good fruit. As leaders of Christ's Church, we are like farmers. God has given us responsibility for preparing the hearts of people to receive the seeds of the Gospel. He has also entrusted us with nurturing their souls so that they might produce the fruit of his Holy Spirit.

How to Lead the Church grew out of my desire to help emerging leaders, like you, to capture and understand the art of organizing a body of believers. Early in my personal journey, I learned these lessons through trial and error. Later, I learned from those who successfully led growing, healthy churches. All of the lessons in this book come from my experience.

I want to walk next to you and offer you step-by-step instruction and encouragement which will improve your skills in leading a local congregation and in planting new churches. Use *How to Lead the Church* as a guide to nurture a growing and healthy body of believers that will, in turn, change lives and produce a harvest throughout the villages and cities in your region.

Sincerely,

Pastor Dale

Dale Hummel
Senior Pastor, Wooddale Church
Eden Prairie, Minnesota, U.S.

AS YOU READ

Remember Your Timothys

As you study *How to Lead the Church,* pay particular attention to the leadership principles contained in each chapter. In the margins provided, write what the Lord is telling you and what you might do to communicate each principle more clearly to your Timothys.

The author has great respect and admiration for The Timothy Initiative (TTI). Every day, through our disciple-making process, men and women worldwide pass on what they are learning to others, with the goal of expanding the Kingdom of God (2 Timothy 2:2).

Our hope is that you will take this guide seriously and will ask yourself not only, "How do these principles apply to me?" but also, "How can I pass them to the next generation of church leaders?"

CHAPTER 1

A Leadership Story

This is a story about a 17-year-old boy named Joseph. This boy had eleven older brothers, a sister, a younger brother and a father named Jacob. His father loved him dearly. You know the story. It's in the Bible.

Joseph's brothers hated him for several reasons:

First of all, Joseph was his father's favorite. Jacob loved Joseph more than any of his other sons. He loved Joseph so much that he made him a beautiful coat with many colors. It made Joseph look like a walking rainbow. The beautiful coat also made his brothers angry. It reminded them that their younger brother was their father's favorite. So they hated Joseph even more.

Also, God gave Joseph many dreams, and he would tell those dreams to his brothers. "One night," he said, "I was dreaming, and we were making bundles of wheat in the field. Your bundles bowed down to my bundle of wheat." In another dream Joseph told his brothers, "The sun and the moon and the stars all bowed down to me." This made his brothers very angry. "Who do you think you are?" they asked. "Do you think that you will be a king someday, and we will bow to you?" Jacob did not like that dream either. It sounded like he, too, would bow down to Joseph. But the father continued to protect and favor the boy.

Finally, Joseph was a godly young man, and his brothers were very wicked. Whenever he saw his brothers misbehaving, Joseph would tell his father, and they would get in trouble. For this and for many other reasons, his older brothers hated Joseph. They hated him so much that they could kill him.

One day, the brothers were watching the family's flock of sheep a long way from home, and Jacob sent his favorite son to check on them. "See if they are behaving or if they are misbehaving, and bring me a report," he told Joseph.

So Joseph put on the beautiful coat his father had given him and went to look for his brothers. Because of his brightly colored clothing, his brothers recognized him at a distance.

"He has that nice coat on," they muttered with disgust. "Let's take it from him, kill him, and throw him into this hole."

"You don't want his blood on your hands," advised Reuben, the oldest brother, "Throw him in the pit, but don't kill him. Maybe he'll starve or wild animals will kill him."

Reuben did not say this because he secretly liked Joseph. He hated his younger brother as much as the others. But Reuben was the oldest. He knew his father would hold him responsible if anything happened to the 17-year-old. Reuben planned to secretly rescue Joseph from the pit and send him home to Jacob.

The brother's agreed. When Joseph walked up, they grabbed him, beat him, took off his beautiful coat, and threw him in the pit.

While they were thinking about what to do next, a caravan of traders appeared on the horizon. The brothers had an idea. "Why don't we sell Joseph to these traders? We'll get some money for our trouble and get rid of this boaster at the same time." They pulled Joseph out of the hole in the ground. When the traders arrived, they agreed to buy Joseph. They put chains on his hands and his feet so he couldn't run away. Then, they took him to Egypt to be sold him as a slave.

Reuben was gone while this was going on. When he returned and learned that Joseph had been sold, the oldest brother had a big problem. What would he tell his father?

The brothers decided to shred the boy's brightly colored coat. They killed an animal and splattered the animal's blood on the pieces of the ruined coat. They brought those pieces back to their father and suggested that a wild beast had attacked the boy.

When he heard this, the father cried and cried, believing his favorite son was dead.

How do you think Joseph felt as he was taken, in chains, from home and as he watched his brothers slowly grow smaller and smaller and finally disappear in the fading light of day?

Would he ask, as the caravan wound its way in the distance, "Why did you do this to me? I'm your brother. You're supposed to love me. Why are you treating me like this?" Would Joseph be afraid? Would he pray to God, "Spare my life . . . please? Get me out of here!"

You are students of the Bible. You know that 17-year-old Joseph and his brothers were the older sons of their father Jacob, also referred to as Israel. Jacob's father was Isaac, and Isaac's father was Abraham. In Genesis 22:15-18, God had promised Abraham that, through his descendants, all the nations of the world would be blessed.

But how could that happen after Joseph's brothers behaved so wickedly, and what dark secrets did these descendants of Abraham carry in their hearts after selling him to slave traders? How could the world be blessed through these men?

Fortunately, the story of Israel's children is not about man's faithfulness but about God's faithfulness. God always keeps a few faithful people and uses them to bring about his promises.

Let's take a look at the rest of the story.

* * *

Arriving in Egypt, the traders sold Joseph as a slave to a man named Potiphar. Potiphar was a powerful man. He was head of the secret police for Pharaoh of Egypt. He had a big house and many slaves.

The Bible tells us that God was with Joseph and that he blessed the house of Potiphar because of Joseph. Potiphar could see this, so he put Joseph in charge of his entire household and all his slaves. Nobody was more powerful in the house except for Potiphar. So although he was still a slave, Joseph had a position with power.

How do you think Joseph felt now? Maybe he felt happy. He might have thought, "Sure, I'm a slave, but I have a job. I have influence. I have power. My master likes me. God is helping me." Maybe Potiphar even gave him a new coat—not colorful like his old one but a coat that kept him warm during the cool Egyptian nights and showed his power to the people around him.

But there was a problem: Potiphar's wife. She saw how handsome and strong Joseph was. She wanted him sexually, and every day she would tempt him. "Come and sleep with me in my bed," she urged Joseph. But Joseph said *no*. "Your husband has put me in charge of everything. I will not dishonor him, and I will certainly not sin against God."

Many times, Potiphar's wife tried to seduce Joseph. Every time he said *no*.

This made his master's wife very angry. One day, when no one was in that part of the house, she again pleaded, "Come and sleep with me." When Joseph again said *no* and turned to leave, she grabbed at his coat. He pulled away and ran out of the house, leaving his coat in her hands. Joseph's coat always got him into trouble, didn't it?

"Help!" she screamed, and the others in the house came running. "The Hebrew slave tried to rape me," she told them. "Look, here is his coat."

When Potiphar arrived that evening, his wife showed him Joseph's coat and told her husband the made-up story.

Believing her, Potiphar became very angry and threw Joseph into prison.

Now how do you think Joseph felt? How would you feel? Sad? Angry? Would you lash out at God? Would you question his will? Would you have a conversation like this with the Almighty? "Why did you let this happen to me? I tried to serve you and obey you. I resisted temptation. But you let this happen to me. I don't understand, God. I try to do my best for you, but you treat me like I am your enemy."

Sometimes, we feel like this. We seek to serve the Lord, and we suffer persecution. We resist temptation, and we suffer for it. Sometimes it seems like God has forgotten about us.

* * *

Think about the story of Joseph. His brothers threw him in a pit and sold him to slave traders who resold him to an Egyptian official. Just as he was beginning to find some success in this new land, he was falsely accused and jailed.

Still God blessed Joseph, and the jailer put the young man in charge of all the other prisoners. Maybe he gave Joseph another coat, to keep him warm inside the cold dark walls of the prison.

Sometime later, two of Pharaoh's court officials were thrown into prison—one was Pharaoh's baker and one was his cupbearer. The cupbearer was like a personal secretary to Pharaoh, and part of his job was to taste the wine and food before Pharaoh drank or ate any of it—in case it was poison. It was a dangerous job, but he also controlled who could come and see Pharaoh.

Both he and the baker did things that made Pharaoh angry, so he threw the two men into prison. They were in prison for a long time—over two years—and Joseph got to know them.

One day, Joseph noticed that the baker and the cupbearer seemed very sad and upset. He asked them why. "We've had very strange dreams," they said.

"Well, only God understands dreams," replied Joseph. "Tell me the dreams, and God will give me the understanding."

First the cupbearer spoke. In his dream, he squeezed new grapes into Pharaoh's cup and put the cup into Pharaoh's hand. Joseph replied, "This means you will soon be restored by Pharaoh to your former position as wine taster." Then Joseph added, "When you are restored, mention me to Pharaoh so that I may be released from prison."

Next, the baker spoke. In his dream, he was carrying three baskets of food on his head, and as he walked, the birds came and ate food out of the top basket—which was meant for Pharaoh. Joseph replied, "This means that Pharaoh will soon put you to death by hanging, and birds will come and eat your flesh."

God had revealed the men's dreams to Joseph. For the baker, it was not good news. Pharaoh was still angry and had him put to death. However, Pharaoh pardoned the cupbearer just as Joseph predicted. Unfortunately, the cupbearer forgot about Joseph, and the Hebrew slave stayed in prison.

Have you ever felt like God forgot you? I have.

Have you ever been lonely or been persecuted for your faith?

Have you ever had to suffer, and you called out to God, but it seemed like God didn't hear you?

Maybe you wondered, "Does God even know who I am or where I am?"

Maybe He only hears the prayers of famous preachers or pastors with large congregations.

These are thoughts Satan tries to put in our minds. He tries to discourage us. He tries to make us feel like we're powerless—that God does not know us or care about us. That's because he is a liar, and he lies all the time.

Don't listen to his lies. God sees you. God knows you. God cares about you. It does not matter how big your congregation is. It doesn't matter if you're in a faraway village. He is with you. His Word says he will never leave you or forsake you. And he was with Joseph in prison.

* * *

Here is the rest of the story. Two more years passed, and Pharaoh had some very strange dreams. In one of his dreams, he saw seven fat cows followed by seven skinny cows. The skinny cows ate the fat cows. In another dream, he saw one stalk of grain with seven bulging heads and another stalk with seven thin and scorched heads. The thin and scorched heads swallowed up the bulging heads. He wondered, "What do these dreams mean?"

None of Pharaoh's wise men could explain his dreams. Then, suddenly, the cupbearer remembered Joseph. He said to Pharaoh, "When I was in prison, a Hebrew slave interpreted my dream." Pharaoh said, "Bring him here."

Pharaoh's servants went and got Joseph out of prison. They washed him up and shaved him, and I think they gave him a new coat. Then they brought Joseph to Pharaoh, the ruler of all Egypt.

"Can you tell me what my dreams mean?" Pharaoh asked Joseph, after telling him about the cows and the bundles of grain. "Only God knows the meaning of dreams," said the slave. "I will be his spokesman."

Joseph continued, "This is what God is saying to Pharaoh. Egypt will have seven years with great harvests and much food. This will be followed by seven years of terrible famine with no food. In the seven good years, Pharaoh, you must save as much food and as much grain as you can, so that in the seven bad years you will have enough for your people."

Pharaoh was amazed at Joseph's words. "Who is wise enough to take care of my people and plan for seven years of emptiness?" he asked. Answering his own question, Pharaoh said, "Only Joseph, the man to whom God reveals dreams, is wise enough."

So this Hebrew slave, who was now 30 years old, was put in charge of all Egypt. To show how powerful Joseph was, Pharaoh gave Joseph another very nice coat—and his own ring. "As long as you have this ring," Pharaoh declared, "you are second in charge of all Egypt. Only I have more power than you."

At that time, Egypt was the strongest nation in the world, so when Pharaoh took his ring, which represented his power, and gave it to Joseph, everyone in Egypt had to bow down to him. What a difference! Joseph went from being a slave in prison to the second most powerful person in the world, and God used Joseph to rescue all the people.

For the next seven years, harvests were so bountiful that Joseph constructed huge buildings to store the extra grain. The following seven years of drought and famine affected not only Egypt but also the countries surrounding it. In those years, Joseph sold the extra grain to his countrymen to keep them alive. He also sold grain to the people of the surrounding countries.

Joseph's family in Canaan was suffering from the drought. His father Jacob sent his brothers to buy grain in Egypt. They appeared and bowed down before Joseph. They did not recognize him because he looked different, but he recognized them. He could have sent them away hungry, as he remembered how harshly they had treated him. He did not. After keeping his true identity secret for a while, Joseph invited his brothers to a banquet and revealed who he really was.

> Genesis 45:3-8 "I am Joseph!" he said to his brothers. "Is my father still alive?" But his brothers were speechless! They were stunned to realize that Joseph was standing there in front of them. "Please, come closer," he said to them. So they came closer. And he said again, "I am Joseph, your brother, whom you sold into slavery in Egypt. But don't be upset, and don't be angry with yourselves for selling me to this place. It was God who sent me here ahead of you to preserve your lives. This famine that has ravaged the land for two years will last five more years, and there will be neither plowing nor harvesting. God has sent me ahead of you to keep you and your families alive and to preserve many survivors. So it was God who sent me here, not you! And he is the one who made me an adviser to Pharaoh—the manager of his entire palace and the governor of all Egypt."

Rather than getting revenge by sending them home without food, Joseph in the Old Testament became a picture of Jesus in the New Testament. He forgave his brothers and explained to them that God had planned everything that happened in order to rescue them. Later, Joseph brought his entire family to Egypt to care for them.

* * *

We can learn three important leadership characteristics from the story of Joseph:

1. **Godly leaders always trust in God's control.**
2. **Godly leaders always remain faithful to God, no matter what happens.**
3. **Godly leaders always do their best.**

1. Godly leaders always trust in God's control. In other words, they believe that no matter what happens in their lives, God is in charge. Joseph must have believed that God was in charge of all things that were happening to him. That does not mean that he understood. It didn't mean that he had no doubts. It didn't mean that he felt no fear, or that he wasn't tempted at times to be angry. But every time he had one of these feelings, every time he was mistreated, he must have prayed silently in his heart. "God, I do not understand, but I believe you are in charge."

Even Jesus suffered. He was beaten, spit on and nailed to a cross. The Bible records his exact words: "My God, my God! Why have you abandoned me?" In many ways, Joseph's life should remind us of Jesus. Even though he faced abuse and punishment for wrongs he did not commit, he always believed that his Father was in control. "Not my will, but your will be done."

As you lead the local church, as you lead a ministry, as you plant new churches, can you accept that God is in control? No matter what your circumstances, will you lead for the Lord? You will go into difficult places and face persecution. If you do not believe that God is in control, you will turn and run.

In times of discouragement:

- Look up to the sky and remember God knows where you are and what is happening to you.
- Claim and pray the promises of Jesus in the Gospel. For example, Jesus said in Matthew 28:19-20 that he will be "with you always, even to the end of the age."
- Ask other believers to keep you encouraged in Christ.

2. Godly leaders always remain faithful to God, no matter what happens. In the story of Joseph, he was always faithful, no matter what his circumstances. When he was thrown into a hole and sold to slave traders by his own family, he was faithful. When he was tempted to engage in sexual sin, he was faithful. When he was forgotten in prison, he was faithful. In all these situations, he could have rebelled, but he chose instead to be faithful. And when he was made the most powerful man in the world, under Pharaoh, he stayed faithful to God.

How about you? Are you committed to being faithful to God? We can talk about leadership and say many things about what it means to be leader, but if you do not first believe that God is in control, and if you are not faithful to God, your leadership will not last.

It does not matter what anyone else thinks. When you and I stand in heaven, we will not answer to a human being. We will answer to God. Have we been faithful?

You must pass this on to your Timothys because it will be hard for them. Teach them the story of Joseph so they will always be thinking about what Joseph did.

3. **Godly leaders always do their best.** Because he believed that God was in control, Joseph could be faithful. As a result, he could always give God his best, no matter what. Joseph gave his best as a slave in Potiphar's home. He gave his best in prison. When he was second in charge of all Egypt, he gave his best to Pharaoh. Are you willing to give your best?

God gave Joseph a great responsibility to lead Egypt for the sake of his people, Israel. What responsibility has God given you? Remember the parable of the talents in Matthew 25. One man received five bags of gold, another two bags of gold, and another one bag of gold. Each man was responsible for what was given to him.

When you go to heaven someday, God will only hold you responsible for what he gave you. Do not look at what he gives to someone else, or you will feel jealous if they have more—or prideful if they have less. Instead, be faithful with what God has given you.

Group Exercise: We studied Joseph as an example of godly leadership. Which of his leadership characteristics will you imitate in your own life and encourage your Timothys to adopt?

____

____

____

* * *

While we're at it, let's consider three more leadership truths:

1. **Leadership is a gift from God.**
2. **Godly leaders are men and women who know what needs to be done.**

3. Godly leaders know that, to get things done, they must use their power of influence.

1. Leadership is a gift from God. It is possible to misuse leadership. There are ungodly people who have the ability to lead, but we're talking here about leadership that God gives us—the spiritual gift of leadership. The Apostle Paul says we must take that gift very seriously.

> Romans 12: 6-8 In his grace, God has given us different gifts for doing certain things well. So if God has given you the ability to prophesy, speak out with as much faith as God has given you. If your gift is serving others, serve them well. If you are a teacher, teach well. If your gift is to encourage others, be encouraging. If it is giving, give generously. If God has given you leadership ability, take the responsibility seriously. And if you have a gift for showing kindness to others, do it gladly.

The Apostle James states that we will be accountable for how we use the gifts that God has given us. (James 3:1) We are like doctors, and the whole world is sick with people dying from sin. They search for hope and truth by worshipping false gods and believing in strange philosophies. Satan has lied and seduced them, but we have the cure—the Word of God.

Leadership is very serious. People's lives are in our hands, and we must be careful how we handle the talents and abilities we have been given.

2. Godly leaders are men and women who know what needs to be done. This is what separates a leader from someone who is not a leader. As you train your Timothys, you must discern whether or not they are leaders. Do they know what to do next? This is of crucial importance in their leadership of the local church. Leaders always think about what to do next. They lead their followers to grow in their faith by teaching God's Word, and they train them how to share Jesus in their culture.

Planting churches is only part of the job. Your Timothys need to know what to do after they plant churches. They must understand how to lead those congregations.

Some have a natural ability to lead. But most of us need to learn how to lead, so we should pray for the gift of leadership. Then we should ask, "Do we hunger for it? Do we exercise it? Do we know what needs to be done?"

3. Godly leaders know that, to get things done, they must use their power of influence. Influence is the ability to move someone else to do something. All of us, as leaders, have the power of influence. People are watching us, and by what they see they will learn how they should behave. The question we must always ask is, "Am I being a good influence?"

Group Exercise: Name godly leaders in the Bible and how they demonstrated leadership.

____

____

____

Name leaders not in the Bible and tell how they influenced you.

____

____

____

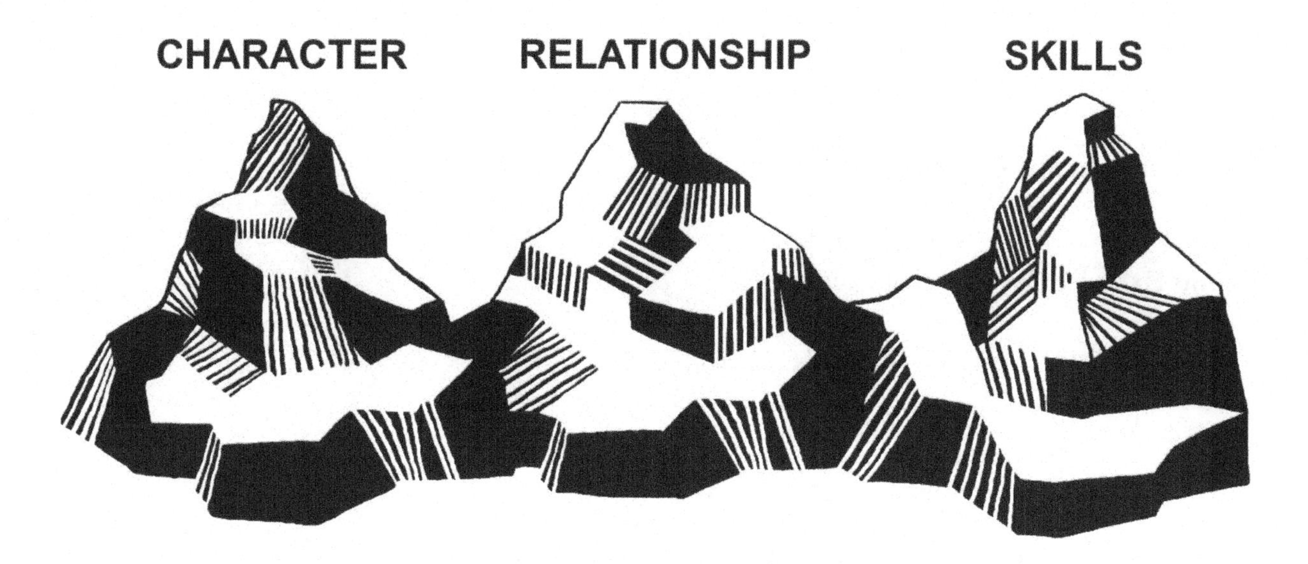

CHAPTER 2

Learning to Lead Yourself

As a Paul, your responsibility is to influence and lead your Timothys. You may also desire to lead your family, your local church, or an organization like The Timothy Initiative (TTI). But first, let me ask you a question, "Who is the most important person you will ever lead?"

The answer is *yourself.* Before you can lead others, you must first learn to lead yourself. You cannot lead others if you cannot, first, lead yourself.

This is a problem among Christians and non-Christians in my country. They want to tell everybody else what to do, but they won't subject themselves to their own teachings. It's particularly a problem for pastors like us.

Before we talk about other practical things to do with leadership, we need to discuss leading ourselves. If we lead our own lives in a godly way, it will change everything else we do. If we're married, we'll become a better husband or wife or better parents. If we're single, we'll become better friends. As pastors, we'll become better evangelists or church planters. We'll improve greatly in our capacity for leadership if we learn to lead ourselves.

To lead ourselves—to become great and godly leaders—we must climb three mountains:[1]

The Mountain of Character

Group Exercise: What is character?

___

___

___

Character is often described as what you do when no one else is watching. We all act like we've got good character when people are watching us, but what happens when nobody is watching us. Then what do we do with our eyes? What do we say with our tongues? What do we listen to with our ears? What do we think with our minds?

Think about King David, for example. The Scriptures call David "a man after God's own heart." Does that mean he was perfect? No, it doesn't. What do we learn about King David's character in 2 Samuel 11-12?

Instead of going to the field with his troops, David stayed behind in his palace. All alone, on the roof of his palace. He looked across to the roof of a house next door and saw a very beautiful, but very naked, woman bathing. David called her over and took her to bed. He committed adultery. Then, when she sent word that she was pregnant, David attempted to cover his sexual sin by having the woman's husband, Uriah, murdered.

David did well in God's eyes, but then he got lazy. The weakness in his character showed itself when he was all alone. If this could happen to David, it can happen to you and me. We have to be careful, because the enemy wants to exploit the weakness in our character and keep us from being effective leaders.

Character truly is what you and I do in secret. Sometimes we do things that are not right, we think things that are not right, we speak things that are not right, and we watch things that are not right when we think no one else sees us.

---

[1] Meyers and Maxwell. *Home Run.*

Throughout the world, one of our biggest problems is sexual sin—especially pornography. It is easy to get, especially on the Internet. Many of our spiritual leaders struggle with pornography.

Being a leader is stressful. We look for relief. Oftentimes our marriages are stressful, so we turn to pornography or a relationship with another person who is not our spouse. We convince ourselves that it doesn't matter. "Who are we hurting?" we reason.

But many men, and even women, become addicted to pornography. Scientists tell us that when a person looks at pornography, it changes their thinking and creates a craving for more. It is a dangerous thing.

Another test of character is how we respond in a crisis or when criticized. When something suddenly goes wrong, and we feel pressured, what thoughts appear in our minds? What comes out of our mouths? Character is not just how we behave when things are going well. It's how we respond when criticism comes.

In America, we have many high-profile pastors. They write books and they're on television. They have many, many followers.

Lately, some of those pastors have had moral failures, or they've made very poor choices in how they behaved under stress. What they have been doing in secret is being revealed to everyone, and it has become a disgrace.

Unbelievers point to these pastors' troubles, and they laugh at the church. They use the sins of these pastors to speak badly about God, making it hard to evangelize. None of us is perfect, but we must work at being consistent in our character. We should be the same at night and under pressure as we are in the good times and in the light of day.

* * *

How then do we develop good, consistent character? We do it by practicing three spiritual disciplines:

1. A Life of Prayer
2. A Life in God's Word
3. A Life of Surrender

Before we continue, it is important for you to understand that prayer and the Word of God cannot be separated. They exist alongside each other. They live and breathe off of each other.

A Life of Prayer and a Life in God's Word

Who talks first, God or me? Most people would say, "It starts with me. I talk to God." But that's wrong. Prayer is responding to what God has already said to us, and although I believe God speaks to us in other ways (vision and dreams, for instance) primarily he speaks to us thorough his Word. I read what he has to say, and I speak back to him. That's why prayer and the Word of God cannot be separated. They are the two primary aspects of communication taking place between us and God.

To show you what I mean by prayer and God's Word being inseparable, let's read the Lord's Prayer in Matthew 6:9-13 (NASB®). Jesus introduced it by saying to his disciples, "Pray, then, in this way:

'Our Father who is in heaven,
Hallowed be Your name.
'Your kingdom come.
Your will be done,
On earth as it is in heaven.
'Give us this day our daily bread.
'And forgive us our debts, as
we also have forgiven our debtors.
'And do not lead us into temptation,
but deliver us from evil.
[For Yours is the kingdom and the power and the glory forever. Amen.']

This prayer was given by Jesus in response to the disciples' request. Luke 11:1 says they asked him, "Lord, teach us to pray, just as John taught his disciples." In the Lord's Prayer, Jesus teaches us the following:

- **First of all, we are to praise God.** "Our Father in heaven, may your name be kept holy."
- **Next, we're to ask God what his will is.** "May your kingdom come soon. May your will be done on earth, as it is in heaven."
- **Then we're to ask God for his provision.** "Give us today the food we need."

- **We are to make confession.** "And forgive us our sins, as we have forgiven those who sin against us."
- **And, we're to deal with temptation.** "And don't let us yield to temptation, but rescue us from the evil one."
- **Finally, we're to glorify God.** "For yours is the kingdom, the power and the glory forever and ever. Amen"

So Jesus teaches that our prayers should have these components: praising God; knowing and doing his will; seeking God's provision; confessing sin; asking God to lead us away from temptation and to deliver us from evil; and allowing us to bring glory to him.

In the past, I've studied larger chunks of Scripture at one sitting. I now read smaller passages of Scripture and go deeper into them. Sometimes, I pour over as few as two or three verses of Scripture and use the components of the Lord's Prayer to understand what God is saying to me.

When I do, I use a chart to organize my thoughts. Here is an example:

Philippians 1:1-2 This letter is from Paul and Timothy, slaves of Christ Jesus. I am writing to all of God's holy people in Philippi who belong to Christ Jesus, including the church leaders and deacons. May God our Father and the Lord Jesus Christ give you grace and peace.

First, I ask, "What is this passage teaching me about how God wants me to **Praise** him?"

As I read and it says *slaves of Christ*, I think of the fact that Jesus is my Redeemer. He bought me. Slaves and servants back then were bought. This is terrible from a human perspective, but Christ bought me with his blood, not to abuse me but to live in me. He bought me out of slavery to sin and into freedom. In Philippians 1:1-2 he tells me, "I want you to praise me as your Redeemer." So opposite *Praise* on the chart, I write "I will praise God as my Redeemer." [See my chart on the next page.]

Let's do one more together.

What is this passage teaching me about **God's Will**? As I read and re-read Philippians 1:1-2, I hear God saying, "I want you to live as my servant. I want you to surrender all your rights to me." So I write down three things: I will live like one who belongs to God. I will live like I am a child of the King. I will live like one set apart, holy to Christ.

That's what I gleaned from those verses, so that's what I wrote down opposite *God's Will* on a chart like the one below.

Scripture Passage ____________________________

What this passage says about:

Praise ____
____
____

God's Will ____
____
____

God's Provision ____
____
____

Confession ____
____
____

Surrender ____
____
____

Temptation ____
____
____

Deliverance ____
____
____

God's Glory ____
____
____

Okay, I think you understand this process. Now, you go on to complete the chart. What is the passage teaching you about **God's Provision**, **Confession**, **Surrender**, **Temptation**, **Deliverance** and **God's Glory**?

Try this in your prayer and study of God's Word. The important part is this. If you want to be a powerful leader and if you want to lead well, you need to hear from God and you need to be talking to God about the things that God wants to happen. One of the reasons why our problems overwhelm us is that we're not communicating with God.

Thoughts on Fasting

I have not practiced fasting until recently. Then it happened. I had a burden for someone, and I felt like God was saying to me, "You need to get back to fasting." So I've been trying to fast one day a week.

I'm certainly not pointing to myself as this amazing example, but I will tell you that it's been wonderful. The time I used to eat, I now give to God. When I fast, I bear down on two things: the desire for Christ to be formed in me and prayer for the things He's burdened me about. It may be for somebody's physical healing or healing of mental illness. God has given me a number of things to soak in prayer when I fast.

Fasting has not been easy. I love food—especially junk food—and I like to snack. But fasting quiets my spirit—and I hear God speaking to me more clearly during those times. I encourage you to try fasting. See if you experience the same intimacy with God that I do.

You might say, "I have low blood sugar. I'm a diabetic. I need to eat regularly." Then try fasting from things other than food. Fast from the media. On the days I fast, I try not to watch any television, and I only use the computer if I need to work on a sermon. I try to block everything else out.

Fasting might be a little challenging if you have a family with kids, so try fasting just half a day at first. For example, block off five hours during which you pray instead of eating. I usually drink juice or water when I fast. But it's the idea of giving up something and putting God in that place. When you fast, you focus more on your relationship and communication with God—and there's a joy that comes with that.

A Life of Surrender

Surrender is not a positive word in any language, but in God's economy it is absolutely necessary and desirable. Surrender refers to submitting entirely to God's perfect and holy will.

For a pastor and church planter, surrender involves practicing the presence of God on a daily basis. As spiritual leaders, it is easy for us to become involved in ministry without first being *with* God. We should want to go out so filled with God's presence that we are like a well—God is springing up out of our lives. That's spiritual leadership. That will accomplish more than anything else we can learn about leadership.

If you are filled with the Spirit of God and you take the tools of leadership, Satan will fear you, and God will do great things through you. But you have to hunger in your soul for God. If you do not, then it's time to get alone with him and ask him to give you back that hunger.

* * *

In the Old Testament, the priest cut the throat of an animal and smeared the blood on the altar, burning certain parts of the animal to make atonement for the people's sins. Jesus died on the cross and gave his blood for our sins, so we no longer have to offer dead sacrifices. However, there is still one sacrifice we are called to make every day. We are called to present our bodies as living sacrifices.

> Romans 12:1-2 And so, dear brothers and sisters, I plead with you to give your bodies to God because of all he has done for you. Let them be a living and holy sacrifice—the kind he will find acceptable. This is truly the way to worship him. Don't copy the behavior and customs of this world, but let God transform you into a new person by changing the way you think. Then you will learn to know God's will for you, which is good and pleasing and perfect.

Worship is not singing, preaching, and going to church. Worshipping God happens when I give my whole life to him. I can express that through music and through a sermon, but the sacrifice begins in prayer by offering myself to God.

Paul's words, translated from the original Greek, can mean "keep on presenting yourself" as living sacrifices. Not just once, but continuously and completely. How do we do this?

Group Exercise: We need a volunteer and a chair. *To the Volunteer:* Pretend this chair is an altar. By sitting on this chair, you are presenting yourself as a living sacrifice to the Lord.

Answer these important questions: "Is every part of your body on the chair? Have you left any part off, like your foot?" Just like you need to put every part of your body on the chair, you also need to present your whole life to God. That includes:

- Your mind
- Your emotions
- Your will
- Your body

To the Group: What did you learn from this exercise?

____

____

____

Sometimes we give our life to God, but we want to keep parts of that life to ourselves. It might be our money. It might be our family. It might be a grudge against someone.

We must place everything on the altar: our minds, our hearts, and our bodies. The Lord wants it ALL as a living sacrifice. This is true worship. This is **A Life of Surrender**.

* * *

What kind of character are you and I supposed to reveal in the good times and in the bad? The answer is that we need to reveal the character of Jesus. In our marriages, each of us must be like Christ to our spouse. As parents, we need to reveal Christ to our children. If we're single and we want to be married, we must look for a man or woman of character, who behaves and talks and acts like Jesus.

People don't need a better you or me. What they need is Jesus.

Likewise, our churches do not need us. The unbelievers in our towns do not need us. They need Jesus living in us and speaking through us. My attitude and your attitude need to be Christ's attitude.

If Jesus is in us, then the people we lead and the people to whom we minister are going to experience God's power, not ours. They'll experience God's presence, not ours, and when they do, many lives will be changed. Miracles will happen, and we'll see unbelievers coming to faith.

Remember what happened in the Gospels when Jesus showed up in a village or town? Five thousand people were fed from just a couple fish and a few loaves of bread. Remember

Zacchaeus, the short man who climbed a tree to see Jesus? He collected taxes and always took more than he was supposed to take. When he finally met Jesus, Zacchaeus gave back what he had taken and more.

When Jesus shows up, he always gives back by changing lives. He gives back a better marriage. He gives back a better family. He gives back broken relationships. When Jesus shows up the deaf can hear, the people who could not talk can talk again, the people who were lame can walk, and the dead are raised to life. When Jesus shows up, peoples' lives change.

What happens when you and I show up?

Unfortunately, we tend to run our churches like businesses. It's about rules, policy, and what we can do in our own strength. The focus needs to be on Jesus and what he can do. Brothers and sisters, listen to me: God wants to walk in your shoes—in you and through you.

Let's look at three verses of scripture together. This is Jesus speaking:

> John 14:12-14 "I tell you the truth, anyone who believes in me will do the same works I have done, and even greater works, because I am going to be with the Father. You can ask for anything in my name, and I will do it, so that the Son can bring glory to the Father. Yes, ask me for anything in my name, and I will do it!"

Those are amazing verses. Listen to what Jesus is saying to you and to me. "If you believe in me," he says, "greater works will you do than I did. You'll ask what you want, and I'll do it." Do we believe that? How can we do greater works than Jesus? Here's a possible answer to that question. When Jesus was on earth, he was one person—in one body. But now he resides in each of us. So in and through us, he can go everywhere. We must change our thinking. God is not asking us to go *for* him but to go *with* him. It is our privilege to be used by him.

Now let's look at another verse. Jesus is speaking again:

> John 4:14 "But those who drink the water I give will never be thirsty again. It becomes a fresh, bubbling spring within them, giving them eternal life."

Jesus says, "When you drink my water (in other words, when you take me into your life) you become like a bubbling spring. It overflows." When it gets hot, how many of us sweat? All of us, right? The water comes out of our skin. In a similar way, Jesus should ooze out of us when we serve others. Let's look at one more passage.

> John 7:38 "Anyone who believes in me may come and drink! For the Scriptures declare, 'Rivers of living water will flow from his heart.'"

Jesus says rivers of water should be coming out of our lives if he is present in us. Listen, whatever ministry you have so far is about to change. Do you believe this? Do you believe that Jesus wants to do more in and through your life than he has so far?

We've been talking about the fact that Christ is in us and Christ is working through us. That means we're not trying to lead the church in our own strength, but his. He's the source of our character, the source of our life, the source of our power and the source of our ministry.

I want us to keep this in mind because most of the time we're trying to minister out of ourselves—out of the principles we learn in classes like this and out of the books we read. But we should want to minister out of his presence. Jesus talks about his life coming out of us like a river, so the question becomes, "Are we like channels that the Spirit of God is flowing out of?"

In Genesis 1, it says "God created mankind in his own image." That means we are imagers of God, agents of God, and ambassadors of God. In Genesis, God invited Adam and Eve and their children to manage the earth—to be partners with him. God said, "Be fruitful and increase in number" and oversee my creation. The Garden of Eden was a small place and God gave Adam and Eve the responsibility to make the whole world like the Garden of Eden. God lived with them in the Garden.

We know what happened, though, don't we? Satan tempted the man and the woman, and they rebelled against God. They were put out of the Garden, and the image of God was marred.

But God came after us and invited us to come back to him. And we do this through Jesus Christ our Savior. In Christ and through Christ we are restored once again to be the image of God and for God to live through us. Once again, we are in partnership with God to bring his kingdom to this earth. The kingdom starts in the hearts of every person.

Testing Builds Character

As leaders, people are drawn to us. The opposite sex is drawn to us, and not always physically. They relate to us emotionally. They think we would be the perfect mate.

Let's look at three passages of Scripture relating to the development of character.

> Deuteronomy 8:2 Remember how the LORD your God led you through the wilderness for these forty years, humbling you and testing you to prove your character, and to find out whether or not you would obey his commands.

Why did God lead the children of Israel though the wilderness for forty years? He did it, according to the writer of Deuteronomy, to test their character, to see if they would be faithful, and to show what was really in their hearts. How did they react? They complained. They worshipped idols, and they tried to kill Moses.

When you are in a crisis, do you respond in anger like the children of Israel? **God leads us into difficult times to show us what is in our heart, so we can repent of it and change**.

As you select your Timothys, do not be in too big a hurry. Make sure they are people of good character.

> Psalm 105:16-22 He called for a famine on the land of Canaan, cutting off its food supply. Then he sent someone to Egypt ahead of them—Joseph, who was sold as a slave. They bruised his feet with fetters and placed his neck in an iron collar. Until the time came to fulfill his dreams, the LORD tested Joseph's character. Then Pharaoh sent for him and set him free; the ruler of the nation opened his prison door. Joseph was put in charge of all the king's household; he became ruler over all the king's possessions. He could instruct the king's aides as he pleased and teach the king's advisers.

God tested Joseph's character. Before his dreams would come to pass and his brothers would bow before him, Joseph would be tested.

In school, I took a class on how to work with metal. One project involved making a metal tool. I had to hold it with tongs, put it in a fire until it was yellow, and beat the end with a hammer to make it flat and sharp. I did this many times, and finally I made a nice screwdriver.

Sometimes God puts us in the heat. **God allows us to go through difficult times, and he uses these trials as a hammer to get rid of our sinful nature and shape our wills, to make us more like him.** That's what he did with Joseph.

> Romans 5:1-5 Therefore, since we have been made right in God's sight by faith, we have peace with God because of what Jesus Christ our Lord has done for us. Because of our faith, Christ has brought us into this place of undeserved privilege where we now stand, and we confidently and joyfully look forward to sharing God's glory. We can rejoice, too, when we run into problems and trials, for we know that they help us develop endurance. And endurance develops strength of character, and character strengthens our confident hope of salvation. And this hope will not lead to disappointment. For we

> know how dearly God loves us, because he has given us the Holy Spirit to fill our hearts with his love.

So, God loves us and God saves us. He puts us through difficult times to develop endurance in us. That's what builds character. We must teach this to our Timothys, but first we must model this in our own lives. Just like Joseph, everything you face has a purpose. God is changing you into the image of his dear Son.

As the Apostle Paul says in this passage of Scripture, the Holy Spirit lives in you. Take your hand and put it on your chest. Do you feel your heart beating? There is a second heart beating in your chest. It is the heart of God, the Spirit of Jesus by whom everything was created. Every believer has a fleshly heart and also the heart of God in their life.

But most of us live by our own power, so our leadership is weak. **If you want to see God change your country, have a great revival and overthrow Satan and the false religions of this land, you must learn to live by the heartbeat of God—not the heartbeat of your flesh.**

God uses difficulties to remove dependence on the flesh so that we cry out, "God, only you, not me. This is the cry of my heart!"

Do you know what the word anointing in the Bible means? In the Old Testament, it means to smear something. When we talk about being anointed by the Spirit, it's like taking a handful of oil and smearing it all over our bodies. We should want God to smear us with his presence within, too.

Who is Keeping You Honest?

Another way we develop character is by seeking accountability. Accountability is making sure we have somebody to keep us honest and faithful. Ideally, I can share my struggles and temptations with that person, and I give them permission to ask me deep questions to help me stay on the right path. Knowing that they are going to ask me these questions helps me stay obedient to the Lord.

Do you have someone like that in your life—someone who can ask you at any time about your marriage, about the sites you visit on your computer, and about your use of bad language? The Bible teaches that we should be open to others.

> Proverbs 27:9 The heartfelt counsel of a friend is as sweet as perfume and incense.

So the counsel of friends is good, and I must give a friend the right to give me advice. For that advice to be helpful, I must be humble and transparent—even to the point of admitting my faults.

> James 5:16 Confess your sins to each other and pray for each other so that you may be healed. The earnest prayer of a righteous person has great power and produces wonderful results.

It is very hard to confess our sins. Sometimes, it is even harder to confess our sins to another person who is sinful like us than it is to confess them to a holy and perfect God. That's because we are afraid of what that other person might think of us. But James says we must confess our sins to a brother or a sister. Only then will we be healed.

PLEASE NOTE: Be very careful who you confess to. The person needs to be a very close friend who you can trust. Someone with whom you can be very open and know they will not spread gossip. Someone you know who will treat you as God treats you—with mercy and grace. That person should also be accountable to you.

Your relationship with your Timothys should be so close that they can share their troubles and their struggles with you and you will not judge them. Instead, you will counsel them and go to God in prayer, and if it is sin, you will help them confess. We all need someone like that to hold us accountable.

The Mountain of Relationship

As pastors, we must develop two kinds of relationships in order to lead. Our Timothys must have these relationships also. The first kind of relationship we've already talked about in The Mountain of Character. That's our relationship with God. The second kind of relationship is with human beings. Let's break down our human relationships into two groups: our families and our leaders. We'll talk about our families first.

Relationships with Our Families

Here's what Paul said is a key qualification for leadership:

> 1 Timothy 3:4 He must manage his own family well, having children who respect and obey him.

Our priority must be our family. As pastors, if we are married, we must be responsible for our spouses and our children first.

Many pastors put the people in their churches ahead of their own marriages and families. This is a sin. The Bible is very clear that we must manage our own households well in order to qualify to take care of God's household. I must be a good husband to my wife. If you are a female pastor, you must be a good wife to your husband. We must both be good parents to our children. Otherwise we are poor examples to our people.

Let me ask you this question. Who is the bride of Christ? The Church (or the people in it) is the bride of Christ, right? So if we are the bride of Christ, who is our husband? Jesus is. As a pastor in the church, I need to be very careful not to make the church my bride. The Church belongs to Christ, not to me. I want the people to depend on the Lord, not on me.

REMEMBER THIS: The Church is Christ's bride. The local church is not your mistress. If you make the local church more important than your spouse, it's like committing adultery, because the Church belongs to Christ. Too many Christian leaders want to own the local church and spend all their time there. That is a sign they are not good leaders. You should always have free time for your spouse. This is a principle you must practice as a Paul, and you must help your Timothys practice it as well.

Let's go a little further into this. Who did we say owns the Church? I'm talking about the people in our congregations, not the building. Christ does. Then, who are the ministers in the church. If you say the pastors, you will be wrong. The members of the church are the ministers. He gives many gifts to different people who minister. *Read Romans 12 or 1 Corinthians 12-14.*

Who are the equippers—the trainers—of these people? We are. The pastors are. Writing to the church at Ephesus, Paul said:

> Ephesians 4:11-12 Now these are the gifts Christ gave to the church: the apostles, the prophets, the evangelists, and the pastors and teachers. Their responsibility is to equip God's people to do his work and build up the church, the body of Christ.

As pastors, we are to lead and train the ministers. We do this in two ways, first by our example and secondly by our teaching and our writings. You are being taught by me today, but I think you also want to see me live and practice what I teach.

Since Christ owns the Church, not the pastor, you and I need to make sure that we are taking good care of our families.

Many pastors around the world do not have good relationships with their families. They struggle in their marriages and with their children. Part of this is cultural. In many cultures, men have been taught to think of women as less important than a man. This is not biblical. Just because a culture says we should view women a certain way does not make it right. The same is true of our children. Certain cultures treat children as less important than adults.

Oftentimes, we want our wives and children to submit to us, but Jesus welcomed the children and treated women with high value. Our wives and children can submit joyfully to us when we truly treat them like Jesus.

So build a strong marriage and a strong family by spending time with your spouse and your children. What good is it if you lead other people to Christ but lose your family? We'll each have to stand before God someday and answer for the priorities we have chosen.

Relationships with Our Leaders

When Jesus came to this earth, he invested his life in 12 disciples, and he spent even more time with three: Peter, James and John. Who are your disciples? Who are the men and women that you are investing in to help you lead the church and plant additional congregations?

You cannot do it all by yourself. If you try, you will become very sick and very tired. You must spread your leadership influence by spending time with other people and training them. So what kind of people should you choose to be on your team?

They must be men and women of character. Choose people who you know love God and want to live holy lives. Some of these may turn on you. This is a risk of leadership. Not everyone is perfect, just as you are not perfect. Not everyone will go the whole journey with you. But you are to prayerfully select men and women who, from what you can tell, do love the Lord.

They must have influence over others. You'll readily recognize those who can get other people to follow and work together. Even in a group of children, you can tell the leaders from the followers. Put the leaders in a room, and the followers will defer to the leaders as to what games to play and the role of each child in that play.

In the same way, you will know the followers in your local church because they will cluster around the leaders. This will help you identify Timothys who will be able to plant and lead new churches.

They must know what needs to be done. Leaders cannot stand still. They must go accomplish something. Choose men and women with the same idea in mind that you have. They may come from differing backgrounds and locations, but they share the same mission and vision with you.

They must be loyal. Choose men and women who will follow you but are not blindly loyal. They trust you but are willing to speak up when they do not agree with something you say or do. They can help you keep on the right course.

* * *

Besides church-planting leaders, you'll need Timothys to care for the people in the local church as it grows. Remember the Book of Acts where it says "3,000 people believed in one day." At first, the apostles tried to take care of these people. They had no time to pray, no time to study, and no time to preach. So they appointed seven godly people to look after the needs of the early church.

Keep some Timothys to help you lead the local church, and select others who will go out and start new churches. As the church grows, teach your people that you are not the only pastor. You have appointed other pastors and lay leaders to help, so you can focus your efforts on leadership development.

Build relationships with both types of leaders, whether they stay with the local church or go out to start new churches. Be open to them personally. Learn about their families and their work. Make it your goal to become friends with your Timothys.

Define your expectations for these Timothys, whether it is to evangelize, to lead worship, to disciple others, to administer or to care for people in the church you lead. Make it clear what you want them to do and, as importantly, what you don't want them to do.

Training Leaders

As we learned earlier, an important part of a pastor's role is to equip God's people for works of service so that the body of Christ (the Church) may be built up.

Use this Four-Step Training model[2] to show prospective leaders and workers how to plant and grow a new church or how to care for an existing congregation. You should be able to train them effectively in any area of ministry by asking them to do these things in sequence.

1. **Watch me** as I do this task.
2. **Join me** in doing this task.
3. **I watch you** do this task.
4. **You're in charge.**

Group Exercise: *With the help of a volunteer, your teacher will now demonstrate the Four-Step Training model.*

To the group: What did you learn from this exercise?

---

[2] Hershey, *The Situational Leader.*

This is a secret of leadership—showing your Timothys how to do something. As the ministry grows, your Timothys will need to find Tituses that they will show how to do it—and so forth.

* * *

NOW LISTEN CAREFULLY: One of the problems we have as leaders is that we have a hard time giving up control. We are fearful that people will think of us as lazy. "They'll think I'm not doing my job," we reason, "and they will stop paying me." THIS IS WRONG THINKING. ***We must train new leaders so we will have time with God, time with our families, and time with our Timothys.*** *This is how God wants the church to operate.*

This is how we must train new leaders who will help us in the local church, as well as those who will plant and lead new congregations. First, we must identify potential Timothys and develop close personal relationships with them. Next, we must make clear what we want them to do and train them by asking them to watch us do the task, by doing the task together, by watching them do the task, and finally by putting them in charge.

Throughout this training process, even after we have put them in charge, we should follow up and be ready to answer our Timothys' questions about the tasks they have been given.

This all takes time, depending on how many Timothys you have. The role of a Paul can be very demanding, so be careful who you chose to spend time with. Always be asking yourself these very important questions:

- **Who do I spend the most time with?**
- **Why do I spend it with them?**
- **What am I hoping for out of our relationship?**

Make sure you are spending time with the right people. There is only one of you. You cannot do everything and serve everybody.

There was only one Jesus, and although he ministered to thousands, he chose to invest his time in 12 people. Out of those 12, he had a close relationship with only three. They walked the roads of Israel together. They ate together. They had fellowship together, and he was always teaching them how to do ministry. After he rose from the dead, he put them in charge.

"Stay here and wait for my Holy Spirit to come and indwell you," said Jesus. "Then tell people everywhere about me—in Jerusalem, Judea and Samaria, and throughout the whole world." [3]

That's what he keeps telling us, too. That's leadership.

The Mountain of Skills

This third mountain represents our strengths and abilities. Let's identify them and talk about how to improve them.

> Ephesians 4:11-13 Now these are the gifts Christ gave to the church: the apostles, the prophets, the evangelists, and the pastors and teachers. Their responsibility is to equip God's people to do his work and build up the church, the body of Christ. This will continue until we all come to such unity in our faith and knowledge of God's Son that we will be mature in the Lord, measuring up to the full and complete standard of Christ. (See also Romans 12:1-8 and 1 Corinthians 12:12-26.)

Group Exercise: List three things God has made you good at and that you enjoy doing. Consider these examples: *music, preaching, teaching, leadership, recruiting, counseling, evangelism, administration, helps, missions, hospitality, building, etc. Can you think of others?*

___

___

___

All of us have strengths—things we enjoy doing. God has given them to us. We should focus most of our energy in the areas we enjoy, because that's what we're good at and how God can use us most.

---

[3] Paraphrase of Luke 24:47-49 and Acts 1:7-8

If we operate out of our weaknesses, we get discouraged. We don't enjoy our work, we tire, and the people don't benefit. This is why I need to look for others with strengths where I am weak, to complement me in leadership.

Perhaps you do not feel gifted in a particular area like counseling. In that case, you need to find someone else who is good at counseling and train them, using the Four-Step Training model. (See page 42) Then you must let everyone know this person has been appointed to do the counseling in the local church.

This is how the body of Christ is to function. We all need each other. But, as we pointed out earlier, so many Christian leaders across the world are afraid to give away ministry. They fear losing control. They teach their local churches something dangerous—to depend more on a human being than on the Lord. Those churches will never accept real leaders, because they have been taught that their pastor is just for them. That is not the case.

God calls us to recognize and make use of other people who have strengths and abilities in areas where we are weak.

Strive to Do Better

Where we are strong, God wants us to improve. For instance, one of my strengths is preaching and teaching. If I did not enjoy preaching and teaching, I would not travel halfway around the world to do it. I've been preaching and teaching now for almost 40 years, but I want to get better. I always want to improve. Here's how I do it.

- **I read about the subject and watch the experts.** By reading about preaching and teaching in books, magazine articles and on-line, I learn from other people who do what I do. (That's what I appreciate about the TTI curriculum. From that set of manuals, you can become a better leader, a better pastor.) And today, with the Internet, there are so many other ways to learn. I also watch people who are better preachers and teachers than me, so I can learn from them. I watch preachers who are better at casting vision or who are more creative, so I can become more creative and better at casting vision.
- **I find someone to mentor me.** A mentor must be someone I can look up to, in whatever I want to do. Find somebody, another pastor or leader, to mentor you. Ask them to help you improve. Your mentor does not have to be older than you, but they

must be better than you at something you want to learn. Do not be afraid to ask for help. *NOTE: As a pastor, it takes humility to ask another pastor to train or teach you.*

- **Finally, I attend seminars like this one.** I'm so proud of you for coming. Thank you for making the effort and sacrifice to be here. I have learned more from seminars than from attending a Bible college, because the seminars featured men and women who are actually practicing what they're teaching. It has changed my life and ministry.

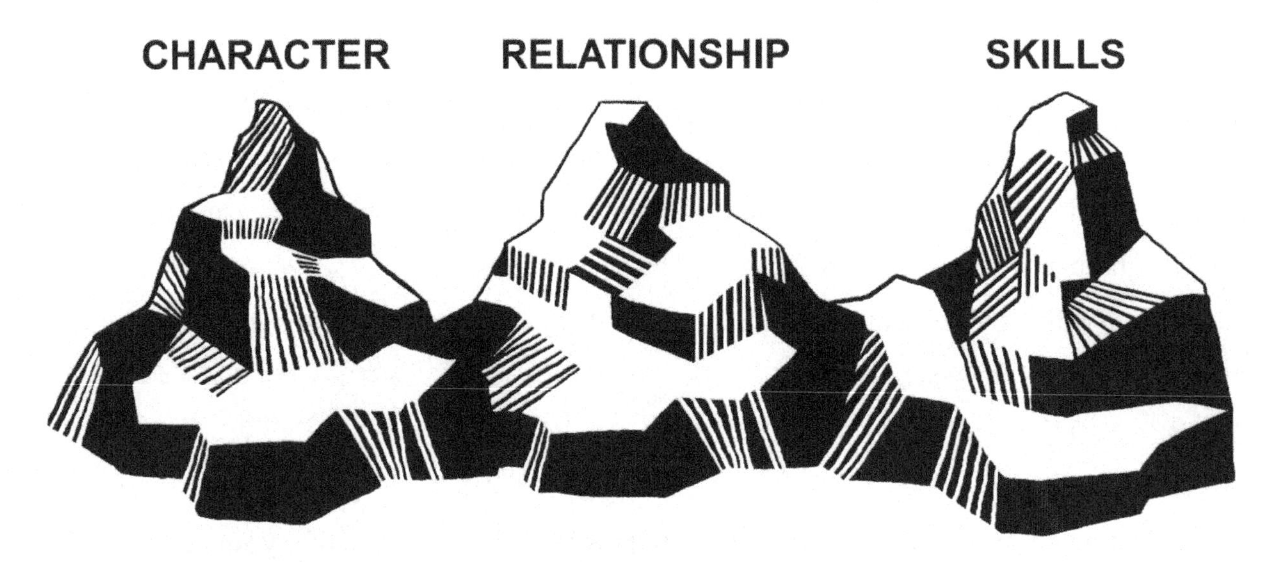

Which Mountain to Climb

In our quest to become great and godly leaders, we've climbed three mountains:

1. **The Mountain of Character** – where we learned to practice A Life of Prayer, A Life in God's Word, and A Life of Surrender.
2. **The Mountain of Relationship** – where we examined our need to develop our relationship with our families, and with others who will help us move the local church ahead. We also learned the Four-Step Training model for developing leaders.
3. **The Mountain of Skills** – where we identified our gifts and talked about ways to make them even better.

Group Exercise: Now, let's all go mountain climbing. Choose between Mount Character, Mount Relationship or Mount Skills. If you had to spend the majority of your time on one of these three mountains, which would you pick?

____

____

____

HERE'S A HINT: If you love revival, prayer, study, and being alone with God, your favorite might be Mount Character. If you like meeting new people and enjoy fellowship, you might choose Mount Relationship. On the other hand, if you love to preach and teach or to make use of other professional strengths and abilities, you might spend most of your time on Mount Skills.

Have you made your choice? Good. Now, this is very important to remember. You cannot stay on just one mountain. **To be a great and godly leader, you must climb all three mountains every day.**

- To start with, **climb Mount Character.** Spend time studying God's Word and in prayer so that, when you climb the next mountain, you have something life-changing to share.
- Then you will be able to **climb Mount Relationship,** manifesting Christ and influencing and relating to people for the glory of God.
- Finally, you will be able to **climb Mount Skills,** using your abilities for God's glory and identifying with the people who will benefit from those abilities.

Again, scaling all three mountains every day will keep you humble, enabling you to share God's love with others and to use the gifts God has given you.

What we have talked about in this chapter is "Learning to Lead Yourself," which is essential to "Learning to Lead Christ's Church." That's our next chapter.

One More Thought

When I ask a crowd of 50-100 pastors and lay leaders how many have the gift of evangelism and love to talk with unbelievers about the Gospel, only a handful raise their hands. But in your country and in mine, we're trying to reach more people with the Good News of Jesus Christ. What does this mean?

In most churches, only a few people have the gift of evangelism. I don't have the gift of evangelism, but that doesn't excuse me from sharing Christ's love with others. It simply means that it doesn't come naturally to me. So I have to work harder at this aspect of ministry and learn how to practice evangelism the way God made me.

Often, we tell everyone else to do evangelism, but we don't do it ourselves. The people in our churches do not respond because they watch their leaders. So if I want the people in my church to do evangelism, then I need to be evangelistic. They must see and hear that priority in my life. In Chapter 6, we'll talk about ways to share the Gospel.

CHAPTER 3

Learning to Lead Christ's Church

Do you know the mission of Christ's church? Do you know the mission of TTI? Can you put your personal mission into words? Many local churches, organizations, and individual believers do not know and cannot communicate *why* they exist. To effectively lead a church, you must be able to clearly state its mission.

The Great Commission, given in the Scriptures below, answers the *why* question. In both cases, Jesus is speaking:

> Matthew 28: 19-20 "Therefore, go and make disciples of all the nations, baptizing them in the name of the Father and the Son and the Holy Spirit. Teach these new disciples to obey all the commands I have given you. And be sure of this: I am with you always, even to the end of the age."

> Acts 1:8 "But you will receive power when the Holy Spirit comes upon you. And you will be my witnesses, telling people about me everywhere—in Jerusalem, throughout Judea, in Samaria, and to the ends of the earth."

Before he ascended into heaven, Jesus gave his disciples the mission for his church, but this instruction went beyond the 12 apostles. It applied to every disciple who will ever walk this earth (you and me included) until Jesus comes again. Jesus said that our mission—the Church's mission—is to take the Gospel message throughout the earth and to baptize and disciple the new believers. Evangelism and discipleship are locked together.

The problem in many local churches is that they have unlocked evangelism and discipleship. They hold up discipleship and forget about evangelism. Evangelism and discipleship are meant to be done together. We cannot be true Christians if we are not also witnessing for Christ. Witnessing is a sign of spiritual maturity.

Group Exercise: What is the mission of the local church you lead? ______________________

____

____

The mission should answer the question, "Why does my local church exist?" The mission is something you must teach your Timothys and model for them. Teach it, as well, to all members of your congregation. As you teach, talk twice as much about evangelism as you do about discipleship, because people don't like to share their faith. They are selfish. They think the church is just for them. It does not exist just for them. It exists for others as well. This is very, very important.

It may be helpful for each local church to adopt a short mission statement to which its leadership refers when making decisions. This statement should focus on both evangelism and discipleship as key parts of the church's purpose.

The local church I lead says it like this: "Our mission is to honor God by making more disciples for Jesus Christ." Discipleship, as well as evangelism, is represented in this statement by the words "making more disciples."

Create your own mission statement, based on words that work best in your language, but remember to lock together the key principles of evangelism and discipleship.

You can express your church's mission in many ways; but no matter how you say it, it must agree with why God says it exists. It needs to be a clear and simple sentence that you often repeat in church. If you do, it will help you and your congregation to evaluate everything you do. You will know which ministries to have and which to say *no* to. On the other hand, if you and your people do not know and declare frequently why the church exists, you make an opening for Satan to lead you in the wrong direction.

NOTE: Many local churches give the right reason for their existence, but don't actually live that way. They haven't won anybody to Christ for a long time. In America, for example, 80 percent of our churches are declining. You've heard of some big churches in the U.S., but did you know there are far more small churches? The average U.S. church has a membership of 75 people. They are small because they don't practice the Great Commission.

Members who have lost their understanding of why their local church exists tend to view themselves as the owners of the church. The pastor doesn't remind them of their mission, and he doesn't lead by example. Instead, he becomes like an employee, existing to take care of the members' needs—cleaning the building, make copies of the music, taking the sick to the hospital, and conducting funeral services. The members of these churches tend to be older, so there are few weddings to perform. The pastor exists primarily for the members. They are his boss.

But the real boss and owner of the Church is Jesus Christ, and the real ministers are the members of the local church. It is the pastor's job to mentor and send them out to bring in more new people. These new believers must, in turn, be trained and sent out. Actually, every person in a local church should be a Timothy. Some will go out to plant new churches and others will stay behind to help build existing congregations, but every believer should be a disciple, and every disciple should be a disciple maker.

To remain true to God's purposes, you must know why your local church exists and you must say it over and over and over again—because every new member who comes in must know why the church exists. People in power may be tempted to use a local church for their own purposes. For this reason, you must establish and reinforce what God says about why churches exist. The church of Jesus Christ exists for no other reason than to fulfill the Great Commission.

The Vision of the Church

Not only do each of us, as pastors, need to answer the question, "Why does my local church exist?" but we also need to answer a second question. "What will my local church look like, at a specific point in time, if we take our mission seriously?" The vision is different than the mission. The mission answers the *why*, and the vision answers the *what*.

If the mission states "We will make more followers for Jesus," then the vision should tell us how many followers we will make and by when.

Here's an example. Traveling to your country to teach, I got on an airplane and the airplane took off. Now, the airline already had a mission which included "flying passengers (like me) around the world." But before my plane was airborne, the pilot filed a flight plan—a vision, if you will—that stated where and when he would land the plane. He also calculated how much fuel it would take to get there.

Most pastors are like pilots without plans. They have no vision for carrying out the mission of their church, so they just go in circles—and eventually they run out of fuel.

What is your vision for your church? Many airplane trips involve two, three or even four stops. Vision is the same. The vision God gives you for your church may involve several different segments. The most important thing is to know where you are going, when you will arrive and what it will take to get there.

For example, if your mission is to reach more people for Christ and help them grow in their faith, and you have 10 people in your church, your vision may not be to reach everyone in your country. But 10 people can grow to 20 people, and you can estimate how long that will take. When you have 20 people, and if each reaches one more person, your church can grow to 40 people, and so on. As you keep going, your vision just gets bigger and bigger.

Have you ever heard this riddle: "How do you eat an elephant?" The answer is, "One bite at a time." That's how you reach your country—with every pastor and every member of every church reaching at least one person for Christ.

Here's an exercise for you. It's a prayer exercise, so I want you to bow your heads. In your mind, I want you to imagine your church as it is today, whether it is five people or 50 people or 150 people. Try to see all of them in your mind. Next, I want you to imagine the building in which you are currently meeting. How many children are there? How many youths? How many adults? Picture in your mind your Sunday worship meeting. See also the neighborhood where your church is located—the people who live around you. Imagine you are up in the air, looking down, trying to get a view of your village or your city.

Now, I want you to ask God to give you a vision of what your church will look like in three years? How many new people do you see? How many children, how many youths, how many adults are there in total? Where are you meeting? What does your worship look like? How will your growing church change the neighborhood, the village or the city? Can you picture that in your mind?

Open your eyes. That's the process of getting a vision. It starts by seeing where you are today and the impact you have on the community, and asking God, "What do you want our church to look like in the future—and how do you want us to get there?"

Vision between You and God

When we talk about casting a vision, it's not something I'm asking you to make up. Everything we talk about begins at Mount Character. It's a spiritual exercise—coming out of a life of prayer, a life in God's Word, and a life of surrender. (See pages 27-33.)

Sometimes we use the term *wrestling with God* to describe how we hear God's will and speak it back to him. We might more accurately describe this as *wrestling with ourselves* until we get to a point where we're yielded to God—to a place of learning to wait on God.

To me, wrestling with God is actually getting to the place where my heart is truly in tune with God. I can hear him speaking to me through his Word, through his Spirit, and through the voices of others who are in tune with him.

As you think about the future of the church you pastor and what it could become over a certain period of time, just remember: it's a flow of ideas and information that starts with God. He expects you to use the abilities he has given you to bring this about.

Size is Not the Focus

I've just asked you to put some numbers down, but I want to make sure you understand that they are important only insofar as they illustrate the growth that can occur if we trust God's Spirit to lead us. Jesus used numbers this way.

In the Parable of the Talents (Matthew 25:14-30) the owner left five bags of gold with the first man, two bags with a second man, and one bag with a third man.

The owner came back and asked the first man, "What do you have to show me?"

"Look, I've doubled what you gave me," said the first man. "You gave me five bags and here are 10 bags." The owner said, "I am so proud of you. Good job. You're a great servant. He came to the next man and said, "How about you?

"I doubled what you gave me," said the second man. "You gave me two and here are four bags. The owner said, "Great job! I'm proud of you." He came to the next man and asked, "What do you have for me?"

"Nothing," said the third man.

"What's wrong with you?" asked the owner, his anger rising.

"I know how hard you can be—that you expect results," stammered the third man. "So I protected the gold—it's safe in the ground."

The owner flew into a rage. "If you knew I was a hard man, why didn't you put it in the bank so at least I'd get interest?'

"Go get it," demanded the owner.

The third man dug up the bag of gold, and the owner snatched it from him. He ordered the third man to leave his presence, and he gave the bag to the man who had 10.

If you will notice, in Jesus' story the amount of gold received by each man differed. Do you think that one of these men was more important to the owner than another?

I don't think so. Just because one man received five bags did not make him more important than the man who received one. It seems that the owner gave to each man according to his ability.

The same is true of you and me. God does not compare us to each other. In fact, I do not believe that God compares me to any other pastor in the world. Other people do. I sometimes do. But that's wrong, because God does not. God says, "I put you where you are and I gave you gifts. Be responsible where you are and with what I've given you."

Some of us are in a very easy place to do evangelism, and some of us are in a very difficult place. Some places where we go a pastor could be killed or put into prison if the authorities find he is a Christian. God expects each of us to do their best with what we've been given. And when we do, as the parable says, he gives us more responsibility.

Prepare for Vision Fulfillment

Jesus also told the Parable of the Talents to remind you and me that he expects us to multiply our ministry, not just by sending Timothys out to plant new churches, but also by bringing unbelievers into the congregations we already lead. If we do not plan ahead, these new disciples will not come, or if they come, we will not be prepared.

Imagine asking a husband and wife in your congregation to host a dinner this very evening for three guests. They agree and begin preparations. Meanwhile, you go out and rent a bus with 50 seats. On the way to the dinner, you stop and invite everyone you see to come and eat with you. When you knock at your hosts' door, you tell them, "Fifty people have come for dinner!"

How will that make your hosts feel? Perhaps they will be angry and embarrassed. If your hosts had known 50 people were coming, they would have gone out to buy more food, and they would have found a room big enough to serve 50 people. They might even have invited family and friends to help them prepare the food.

The same is true of the local church. We must plan for the church to grow so we can accommodate new people and so that these new people will be welcomed. We must always think ahead. That is why we must cast a vision as well as remind the congregation of its mission.

A Plan for Church Growth

ADOPT 7 is a three-step method for sharing Christ with an unbeliever. It also provides a framework for planning the growth of a local church.

Before you begin, think of seven people with whom you come in contact on a regular basis who you know are not Christians—or at least you are not sure. Write down the names of these people. They could include a clerk at the market where you buy vegetables, the person who puts petrol in your car or motorcycle, someone you work with, your doctor, your neighbor, or a family member.

This exercise may be harder for someone who has been a Christian for many years than for a new Christian. The longer a person is a believer, the fewer non-believers they know. But Jesus did not spend all of his time with religious people. "It is not the healthy who need a doctor, but the sick," he says in Mark 2:17 (NIV®). "I have not come to call the righteous, but sinners."

Many people you know will be receptive to the Gospel message. You must reach them with Christ's offer of spiritual healing. So, ADOPT 7. Then, take these three steps: 1) Pray for them. 2) Serve them. 3) Share Jesus with them.

1. Pray for them. Every day, pray for the seven. Each time you see one of your ADOPT 7, pray for them to come to Christ.

2. Serve them. Go out of your way to get to know each one on your ADOPT 7 list. When you see them, stop, shake their hands, and help them with whatever they are doing. Look for any need they might have and try to fill it. Invite them to your home for a meal. Eventually, you will become their friend. This may take a while, perhaps years in some cases, but do not give up.

3. Share Jesus. As you love and serve them, they will eventually become your friends and will begin to ask why you are so different. Share with them what Jesus did for you. Present your testimony in three parts: What your life was like before meeting Jesus. How Jesus found you. How Jesus has changed your life.

Then ask them, "Could I share with you how Jesus could change your life?" If they say *yes*, you will have the opportunity to share the Gospel with them. If they choose to become a new Christian and part of God's family, then encourage them to also ADOPT 7 and introduce more people to Jesus.

If they say *no*, don't take it personally. Continue to be their friend and care about them. They may be testing you to see if you really do care about them or if you are just trying to make another Christian. Jesus did not die only for those who would turn to him. He died for everybody, even the soldiers who pierced his side.

Finally, realize that you may plant the seed and reap the harvest by seeing a friend accept Christ, or you may simply be privileged to plant a seed that you will never see ripen. Someone else may witness that person's decision. The important thing is that we're planting seed and praying for our friends to eventually come to faith.

Group Exercise: Now let's see what ADOPT 7 looks like. We need several volunteers. One person stands in the middle and the rest make a circle around him. Face him, stretch out your arms, and rest your hands on his shoulder. *Your teacher will lead you through this exercise.*

To the Group: What did you learn?

____

____

____

Evangelism is loving people like Jesus loved and earning the right through friendship to give them the Gospel message. People will be attracted to Christ as they see you practicing what you preach. In the end, it is the Holy Spirit's job to convict them and bring them into a saving relationship with Jesus Christ. Your job is simply to pray, to serve, and to share. Will you ADOPT 7?

PASTORS: ADOPT 7 is a good way for you to figure out your vision for the church. Let's say you each have 30 people in the churches you pastor and each of them prays for, serves and shares Jesus with seven believers, they have a potential to reach 210 people who could each ADOPT 7 more.

Do you see the principle of multiplication at work here? If you can get each of your people to ADOPT 7, it could change your villages, your cities and the whole country.

This is part of the vision you will want to give your entire congregation, and the best way to do it is to be honest about how you are trying to do evangelism. That's because people learn by example.

Teach this to your people, encourage them to ADOPT 7 and prepare them to share their testimony with others. Unbelievers can argue with you about religion, but they cannot argue with your personal experience.

Every Sunday have one or two of the believers in your congregation practice sharing their personal testimonies with the entire congregation. This will help them get used to sharing their testimony with someone who does not believe.

God Plans and So Should We

Before we talk about how to carry out a vision, I want to address the mistaken idea that all we must do is pray and God will bring about the growth.

A farmer doesn't sit in his house in the spring and pray, "God, please make many tomatoes appear in my fields." He understands that he must plan and organize his work. He must till the ground, buy the seed, plant it, fertilizer it, cultivate it, harvest his crop of tomatoes and sell it. In doing this, he follows the pattern of his Creator.

Yes, the farmer prays for wisdom, for rain and for sunshine, but he must also do his part. And God does his.

Some concepts we're discussing, like mission and vision, are mimicked in government and business. Does this make them wrong? No. God created everything that is good and pure. He is not a God of disorder, as Paul points out in 1 Corinthians 14:33. All we have to do is look at how wonderfully he ordered creation. The universe is mathematically fine-tuned. God is a God of organization. He has a plan.

Likewise, God gave us brains to use and abilities to exercise. As we lead the church, he expects us to use all that he has given us. God want us to plan and organize.

Roles in the Church

Now let's talk about the roles necessary for a local church to plan, organize and carry out its vision.

The New Testament Book of Acts introduced a team structure that functioned well in first century Jerusalem and works well today, too. Within this structure, three basic roles assume different responsibilities. Unlike a caste system, the people occupying these roles are considered of equal worth and importance to the success of the team.

1. The *leader* says, "This is where we should go."
2. The *manager* says, "I will organize us so we can go."
3. The *workers* say, "Show me the path, and we will go."

Group Exercise: Imagine our mission today is climbing mountains. To achieve our mission, we'll need a leader and two managers. The rest of us will be workers. *Your instructor will set up this exercise and guide you through it. Make notes of what you learn.*

____

____

____

Our leader laid out his vision, but could not climb the mountain alone. The leader needed managers to organize the journey, but the managers could not carry all the supplies up the mountain. They needed each individual worker to carry a specific bundle. In the same way, the workers needed the managers to show them what to bring and the managers needed the leader to show them what mountain to climb. The cooperation of all three roles made it possible for us, together, to fulfill our mission of climbing mountains.

That is very much like how the early church operated. In Acts, the apostles (the leaders) chose seven people (the managers) to oversee the distribution of provisions among the early Christians. The people under them (the workers) actually dispersed the money and the food.

Consider implementing this team structure in your local church. As Paul points out, the Holy Spirit has given each person different gifts and abilities that function with equal importance to the whole body of believers.

> Romans 12:4-5 Just as our bodies have many parts and each part has a special function, so it is with Christ's body. We are many parts of one body, and we all belong to each other.

The pastor (leader) sets the direction for the local church to go, but a pastor cannot do it by himself. He needs others in leadership (managers) to help him organize, and members (workers) who will perform the individual tasks. Then the church can climb any mountain and carry out any vision God gives it.

CHAPTER 4

The Leader and Change

Every time a local church plans, organizes and carries out its vision, change must happen. Adding more people stirs the tranquil waters of our fellowship. We must get used to new people who think differently and who have new ideas. They challenge us, and although this isn't a bad thing, it does require us and the church to go through the process of change. Change is hard.

Our local churches must change. If not, we'll become inward-focused rather than outward-welcoming, as the Great Commission requires. New people will come, and if they don't feel welcome, they will leave. There are many churches that stay small because they are like a family. They won't let anybody new in.

Group Exercise: We need volunteers to stand and form a circle, facing inward with interlocked arms. Let's pretend these are a local church. Visitors approach the church, trying to get in to meet Jesus. *Your teacher will lead you in this exercise.*

To the group: What happens when the visitors try to get in?

____

____

____

____

What happens if church members face outward with unlocked arms extended outward?

____

____

____

____

Think about your church right now. Does it look like the circle with everyone facing inward with interlocked arms? Does it function like a family that is unwilling to admit anyone else? Or does your church face outward with their arms open, welcoming others in? As long as you keep your church outward-welcoming, it will grow because your members are open to unbelievers.

The way to stop a church from turning in, from the beginning, is to keep the members evangelizing.

Convincing the Church to Change

Change is good if it helps us welcome and disciple new believers. But how do we, as leaders, convince local churches they need to do things differently?

Nobody likes change. We all like things to remain the way they are. That's a problem, because God loves change. First of all, his Spirit is in the process of changing us. None of us is perfect yet. But God sees us as perfect because Christ lives in us, and his perfection is also being released in us day by day. We call that *sanctification*. Our lives should always be changing as we become more and more like Jesus. The Bible teaches that we will not be complete until we get to heaven.

There's another reason God prefers change over tranquility. When Israel entered the Promised Land and finally settled in it, the people committed idolatry by worshipping Baal and Asherah. If you study those two gods, you'll learn that it was really a worship of the land. Israel worshipped what God gave them instead of the God who gave it. The danger, when we don't change, is that we begin to worship our circumstances. We stop moving with God in favor of preserving our comfort.

It is easy to commit idolatry with our church buildings. Buildings are comparable to the land Israel worshipped. For instance, God wants us to grow, to change lives, and to accomplish the vision he's given us. But if the church is too small and there is no room for the number of people showing up for worship, we may need to move—to worship in two places or find a bigger building. This building may be further away, and the people worshiping now many not want to travel that far. If we divide into two congregations, we may have to meet new people, and that might make us feel uncomfortable. Maybe we'll have to leave good friends behind, and that might make us sad. In some parts of the world, moving to a bigger building may also upset the authorities and give them cause for persecution of Christians.

The temptation is to stay quiet and stay where we're comfortable—where we're worshipping now.

It is also easy to commit idolatry with our Christian friends. My wife Marcia and I were pastoring a church in a place called California. I was teaching the church members about the importance of evangelism. In that church, Marcia and I belonged to a small group of believers. We studied the Bible together, prayed for each other and had fellowship together.

At the same time, God told Marcia and me to begin evangelizing some people outside the church. Because we started spending time with these unbelievers, our Christian friends began to draw away from us. They did not appreciate that fact that we were dividing our time and attention between them and the non-Christians. They wanted us to stay in their tight circle, like a family, and not let anyone else in. This hurt us deeply.

Let me ask you a question. Is it better to help Christians grow in their faith or to reach out to non-believers? Do you remember the example Jesus used? A man had 100 sheep. One was missing. Should he stay with the 99 or leave them and go look for the one? He goes to find the one, doesn't he? So while both are important, going after the lost matters more.

In the second chapter of Mark's Gospel, Jesus said, "It is not the healthy who need a doctor, but the sick. I have not come to call the righteous, but sinners." [4]

We must teach our people to do the same.

Turn to the next page. →

---

[4] Mark 2:17 (NIV®)

Pastors are not exempt from idolatry. Compare the pursuit of a God-honoring vision, like growing a local church, to climbing a mountain. A climber reaching the peak is understandably excited. A pastor achieving a vision may share the same excitement over a worship center full of believers, Bible studies, women's groups, children's classes, and abundant offerings. The climber may be tired after his ascent. The pastor, too, may experience fatigue after achieving a vision and be tempted to get lazy. Success is a very comfortable place to rest in.

With nowhere else to go, a climber must eventually come down the mountain. Likewise, without a new vision, the successful local church will eventually decline. People will grow old and die, or move away. Disagreements between the pastor and a membership in decline often result in church splits. The pastor may be able to keep the remaining people happy for a time, but sooner or later that church will die.

It's important to know when it is time to cast another vision and climb another mountain.

A Story about Change[5]

In the jungle grew a very tall coconut tree and under that tree there was a village of about 50 people. They had lived there for a very long time. The land around the village was slowly losing its ability to grow sweet potatoes, and the tribe had killed and eaten most of the animals in the surrounding forest. As their food sources dwindled, the village people remained content with their lives under the coconut tree—all except for one, the chief.

The chief was always thinking about the future. He knew the people he led had lived in one place too long. It was hunted out and the soil was worn out. The tribe needed to move.

One day, the chief climbed the coconut tree and looked out over the forest. Twenty or thirty kilometers away, he saw a wonderful place the villagers could move to. He saw high ground where they could build their huts. Nearby was nice flat ground where they could plant sweet potatoes. He also saw a river where his people could fish, swim, and wash their clothes, and he saw many animals they could hunt.

"I must get the villagers to move there," thought the chief, "but that would mean packing up all our things and moving a long distance. It would require a lot of work, and the people of the village like where they live right now."

The chief climbed down the tree, stood before the villagers, and began his speech with these words. "We must move our village." He explained all the reasons for moving and described the beautiful land he had seen from the top of the coconut tree.

"No, no, no!" the villagers responded angrily. "We will not move!"

"We like it where we are."

"We have raised our children here, and we know this land."

"We don't know the land you are talking about."

"We have built houses here. We don't want to take them apart and move to where other tribes may fight us or diseases may kill us."

"You are crazy. There are many of us and only one of you."

"No, no, no," they chanted in unison. "We're staying right where we are!"

---

[5] Borden, *Hit the Bullseye.*

The chief and his
warriors climb the
coconut tree.

Sad but still determined, the chief considered what to do next. Then he had an idea. The chief of every village had warriors. These warriors had power and influence. They had families and friends in the tribe, but they were loyal to the chief. The chief met with them on a regular basis. They hunted and fished together. They trusted one another.

The chief said to his warriors, "Climb to the top of the coconut tree with me." The warriors followed their chief up the tree.

When they arrived at the top, the chief said to his warriors, "We need to move. You and I both know we're running out of food, and if we stay too long there will be no food. We'll starve, and by then we'll be too weak to move."

"But," he said, directing their attention to the hill in the distance, "I see a new place where our village would flourish. Do you see it?"

The warriors look over the forest to the hill. "Yes, we see the high ground," they said. "Let's build our huts there. Look, there is some very nice ground to grow our crops, and there is a river where we can catch fish, our children can play, and we can draw water to drink. There are also many monkeys in the trees and other creatures on the ground that we can hunt."

Then the chief spoke again. "We have a problem," he said. "Our people have become too lazy and accustomed to living here. They do not want to move. We must help them."

So the chief and his warriors climbed down the coconut tree, and the warriors made the people move their village with the sharp points of their spears. "Move or else," they said.

Group Exercise: We need volunteers, one to play the chief and the others to be his warriors. All the rest of us will be the villagers. Let's stand and pretend the chief has ordered his warriors to move us to a new location with the sharp points of their spears. *Your teacher will show you how.*

To the Group: What does that feel like? Will we move? Will it be good for us?

____

____

____

Except for the spears, this story is remarkably similar to the situation in which many local church leaders find themselves today. Their people are growing older and have turned inward.

There are fewer and fewer young families joining these churches because they do not feel welcomed. The members like things just the way they are and do not want to change. They may not realize it, but they are very close to starving for the next generation that will lead their churches. By the time they come to their senses, they may be too weak to change.

Like the chief in the story, the pastor of the local church described above may have warned his congregation. He may have tried to make changes that would open the church to new people, but the members said, "No, no, no!"

Now, what can he do? The answer is clear. He must show his vision to his warriors—the elders and deacons with whom he spends time and who trust him.

In the local church, of course, we don't use spears to make people do what they should do. Instead, each of the pastor's warriors has a tool they can use. It's called *influence*.

These lay leaders know the people of the congregation. Some are family and friends. They can sit down to dinner or tea with the people they know and explain why the local church needs to change. They can conquer a church full of people, one heart at a time.

Group Exercise: Now we need the same volunteers to play the pastor and the elders in the local church. This time, move the congregation, not with spears but with a handshake and conversation with people they know who will, in turn, tell others. *Your teacher will demonstrate.*

To the Group: What does that feel like? Will we change? Will the change be good for us?

____

____

____

Reasons for Change

One thing that brings about change in a local church is a crisis. In some churches, the crisis is the rising average age of the members and not enough children. That's a crisis. If you don't have a ministry that reaches children, the church will at some point close its doors.

Another kind of crisis occurs when somebody decides to teach something that is not true. You must confront them and tell them they cannot teach this way. They may not repent. They may argue and challenge you, but you must stand on the truth. They may leave and take other believers with them. Let them go.

New people will take their place. With new people come new ideas and new ways of doing things. Rather than being resentful, be thankful.

Still another way a leader can help the local church change is to show them a better picture of the future. Show them they don't have to keep doing things the way they've always done them. There is a better place for them—in their worship, in their attitudes, in reaching their neighbors for Jesus, and in planting new churches. Always keep this picture in front of your people.

Anyone who would lead Christ's Church must have a desire for a new future. Let the vision you created inform the changes you need to make. List them below:

- ☐ ______________________________
- ☐ ______________________________
- ☐ ______________________________
- ☐ ______________________________
- ☐ ______________________________
- ☐ ______________________________

A leader lives in today but also lives in the future and knows how to move the local church from here to there.

Some Things Cannot Change

As a leader, you must know the difference between what can change and what cannot change. For instance, the local church must remain Christ-centered and focused on what the Bible says. The church must also be outreach-oriented as well as providing a place for people to grow and mature spiritually. So make a short list of values that cannot change.

Group Exercise: Write down seven Biblical values every local church should have.

1. ______________________________
2. ______________________________
3. ______________________________
4. ______________________________

5. ____
6. ____
7. ____

If someone makes a suggestion that opposes any of these values, you should be able to go right to Scripture and show them why that suggestion is wrong for the local church.

Values are like the fence around a property. They keep bad influences out and everything inside safe.

Tips for Effective Change

Many times, it is easier to start by changing the smallest thing first. Avoid big changes that might upset many people. Let them get used to your vision gradually by making minor adjustments at the beginning.

Make sure your lay leaders have already agreed with you about the change. Remember the warriors? When they embraced the chief's vision, it was the warriors who influenced the village to move. In the same way, your Timothys will share your vision and will influence the local church. Below are three more tips for effective change:

1. Think of every argument that people will give you for not changing and how you will respond to it.
2. Talk about the positive results of a change.
3. Think far enough in advance that you know what will need to change first, second, etc.

It's a big job to be a pastor or a lay leader, isn't it? There are many things for which we must be responsible. We must lead ourselves. We must lead Christ's church. We must lead change.

CHAPTER 5

The Leader and Encouragement

One of the most important things we must do, as leaders, is to encourage our brothers and sisters in Christ. We live in a discouraging world that promotes accumulating all we can for ourselves, even at the expense of others. Our God teaches the opposite.

> Hebrews 10:24-25 Let us think of ways to motivate one another to acts of love and good works. And let us not neglect our meeting together, as some people do, but encourage one another, especially now that the day of his return is drawing near.

The writer of Hebrews calls us to think of ways we can inspire and motivate each other to further the work of God on earth. One of the ways we can do that is by encouraging one another.

Leading the local church involves knowing how to treat people and how to work with them. Learning this takes time. Overseeing people does not come naturally for everyone. However, you can do three things right now to encourage those you lead.[6]

First, get to know your people. Memorize their names, the names of their spouses, and the names of their children. Find out what is most important to them. Ask about their greatest joys and their heaviest burdens.

In a small church, this should be easy. In a large church, start by becoming friends with your Timothys. Then move to the next level of leadership.

Show that you value them by listening to their story and ministering to them in some tangible way. The people you lead should never feel alone. They should know you genuinely care for them. **Instead of viewing you as their pastor or boss, they should see you acting like Jesus, who put aside his own interests for all of us.**

---

[6] Lencioni. *Three Signs Miserable Job.*

> Philippians 2:1-4 Is there any encouragement from belonging to Christ? Any comfort from his love? Any fellowship together in the Spirit? Are your hearts tender and compassionate? Then make me truly happy by agreeing wholeheartedly with each other, loving one another, and working together with one mind and purpose. Don't be selfish; don't try to impress others. Be humble, thinking of others as better than yourselves. Don't look out only for your own interests, but take an interest in others, too.

Second, tell your people what they are doing is making a difference in the life of the local church and in the world as a whole. Everyone wants to know that what they do matters, whether they lead someone to Christ or wait on tables. The stories below describe both scenarios.

At a house church in the suburbs of Delhi, India, the pastor asked a fifteen-year-old boy to stand and be recognized by the congregation for leading fifteen of his friends to Christ. That young boy had only been a Christian for two months.

The Bible says God rejoices and the angels sing over the salvation of one lost soul. Shouldn't we celebrate these joyous occasions in similar fashion?

Another story: On a wintery morning in February, while the sky was still dark, a big man named Ken arrived at a North American church to brew coffee. Ken was in his 60s, single and very grumpy—he would hardly speak a word. But every Sunday morning at about 5:30 a.m. Ken would show up and make many, many liters of coffee and tea for a church of 3,000 people.

Ken had few friends but had been making coffee at this church for many years. After preparing the delicious hot liquid, he would sit silently among the worshipers. No one knew him and nobody, except for the pastor who also arrived early, had seen him make coffee.

"I need to get to know this man," thought the pastor, so he entered the kitchen where Ken was working. At first all the pastor said was "Hello." Sometimes Ken would mumble a greeting. Sometimes he would say nothing. But because the pastor kept greeting him, he eventually returned the *Hello*.

Next, the pastor made it his mission to put a smile on Ken's face. Soon, Ken and the pastor began talking. Ken told the pastor about his job, his struggles and his loneliness. The pastor listened and told Ken about himself. Then one day, the two men had this conversation.

As Ken finished brewing a big pot of coffee, the pastor stated. "You may be one of the most important people working at our church," he said.

"Me?" said Ken. "All I do is make coffee. You preach sermons and travel around the world. What you do is more important than what I do."

"That's not true," said the pastor, who lived and preached most of his sermons in a cold climate where people wear coats, hats and gloves. "When you provide all the coffee and the tea, it warms people up and helps them become acquainted with our guests who do not yet know Christ."

"When the guests come in," the pastor continued, "your coffee and tea make them feel welcomed."

"Furthermore," joked the pastor, "when everyone drinks the caffeinated drinks you prepare for them, they stay awake when I preach. So, you make a very big difference."

Hearing this made Ken happy and more than willing to serve.

But Ken heard something else, as the weeks went by. He heard the pastor talking about his desire to share Christ with others and to go to countries around the world to share Christ and train pastors. The church was raising money to make that possible.

One Sunday morning, when the pastor arrived at the church, Ken met him at the door of the kitchen. "I no longer have a place to live," said the volunteer, adding, "I moved out of my apartment."

"What happened?" asked the pastor, concerned for his friend. "Can we help you pay the rent?"

"No," said Ken. "I gave up my apartment so I could take the money that I was spending on rent and use it for missions."

"I live in my car now, and when it's really cold, I go to a place where there are other homeless people just like me, and I am with those people," said Ken, smiling. "Pastor, I can minister to those people now."

Ken was happy. He had made a great sacrifice so that his little bit of money could be used to reach people for Christ—both at home and around the world.

The pastor (that man was me) was very humbled. Ken had given a great gift before the Lord.

Do you see what had happened? Because that pastor had made it his mission to get to know Ken and to help him see the difference he was making—the man who "just made coffee and tea" had decided he could do more.

The larger your staff, the more you as a leader need to encourage them and let them know you care. People would rather work for someone who tells them "I'm so glad you are here—what you do is changing the world" than for a person who barely acknowledges them.

That's real motivation.

Finally, let your people know that you expect a little more. In other words, help them think about how they might perform their ministry even better.

"I want to challenge you to do something," you might say. "I know you have many responsibilities, but I need you to develop three new leaders who will take some of these responsibilities from you, because I need to give you a greater responsibility."

"I know you can do it," you might add, assuring them of your confidence. "Will you give it a try?"

Then, when they do as you have requested, be ready to reward them—not with money but with praise or by inviting them to have coffee or tea with you. You pay for it.

People appreciate small rewards. They like something to work toward.

In his first letter to the Corinthians, Paul says we will be rewarded when we get to heaven. We do not earn salvation. That is given to us by God's grace, but we are rewarded by how we live and work for the Lord. So think of how you can encourage and reward the people you lead as they work for the Lord on this earth.

Group Exercise: *Break into small groups and answer these three questions.*

Are you a good encourager? ____

What encourages you? ____

How could you do a better job of encouraging those around you? _______________

____

PLEASE NOTE: If you are a shy person, as opposed to an outgoing person who likes to be with other people, you may need to work harder at being friendly. If you work at it long enough, however, you will learn to encourage others.

CHAPTER 6
The Leader and Systems

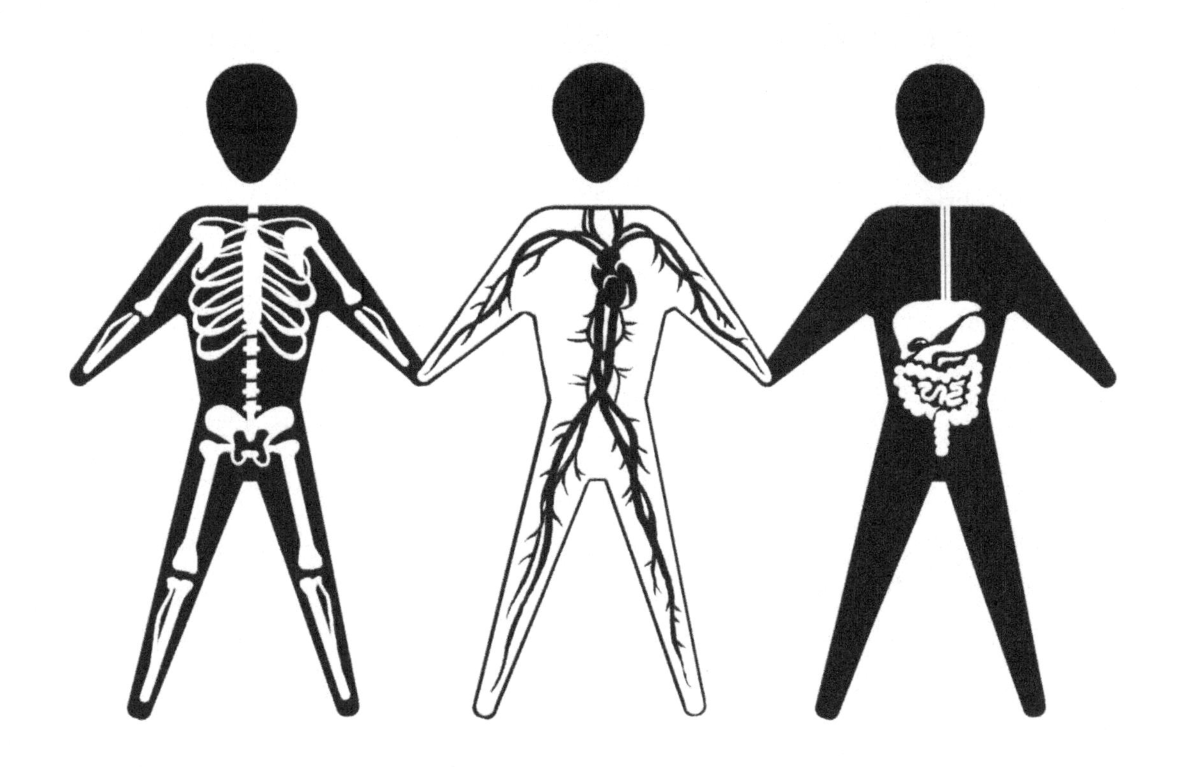

Various systems make up the human body.

For instance, feel the bones in your hand. You have bones throughout your whole body. Medical science calls this your *skeletal system*.

Throughout your body, you have muscles that move those bones. Doctors refer to this as your *muscular system*.

Then, too, you have arteries and veins carrying blood throughout your body. This is known as your *circulatory system*.

Your body also contains a stomach and intestine called your *digestive system* to take in nutrients, and an airway and lungs called your *respiratory system* to take in oxygen.

God made our bodies to operate with the help of the systems above. When one of these systems is not working, you go see a doctor.

In the same way the Church, which God calls the body of Christ, is made up of systems. As a pastor, you're like a doctor. Your job is to make sure all the systems are healthy and working.

As a smart pastor, you should appoint leaders over each system. If you don't, the church you pastor will stay small because you will become very tired attending to all these systems. If you delegate, however, you will have time to plant other churches—and spend the time God expects you to spend with your family and your spouse.

So what are the systems of the local church? I suggest that there are seven:

1. Evangelism
2. Assimilation
3. Worship
4. Discipleship
5. Care
6. Stewardship
7. Leadership

Let's talk about the first system.

Evangelism as a System

By some estimates, over two-thirds of the world's 7.8 billion people are dying in their sins. We cannot close the door to these lost people.

You are called by God to lead evangelism in the local church. The word evangelism comes from a Greek word *euangelion,* which means good news or Gospel. So it is our responsibility to bring this good news to people.

In his letter to the Romans, Paul calls the Gospel "the power of God".

> Romans 1:16-17 For I am not ashamed of this Good News about Christ. It is the power of God at work, saving everyone who believes—the Jew first and also the Gentile. This Good News tells us how God makes us right in his sight. This is accomplished from start to finish by faith. As the Scriptures say, "It is through faith that a righteous person has life."

What is the Good News? Paul says, it's the power of God to save. It's the story of what Jesus did on the cross. Now let's turn to Matthew and see what Jesus said about the power of the Good News.

> Matthew 16:13-20 When Jesus came to the region of Caesarea Philippi, he asked his disciples, "Who do people say that the Son of Man is?" "Well," they replied, "some say John the Baptist, some say Elijah, and others say Jeremiah or one of the other prophets." Then he asked them, "But who do you say I am?" Simon Peter answered, "You are the Messiah, the Son of the living God." Jesus replied, "You are blessed, Simon son of John, because my Father in heaven has revealed this to you. You did not learn this from any human being. Now I say to you that you are Peter (which means 'rock'), and upon this rock I will build my church, and all the powers of hell will not conquer it. And I will give you the keys of the Kingdom of Heaven. Whatever you forbid on earth will be forbidden in heaven, and whatever you permit on earth will be permitted in heaven." Then he sternly warned the disciples not to tell anyone that he was the Messiah.

The Gospel is the story of Jesus' life, death, and resurrection. When his Church believes that and shares that by witnessing, by evangelism, it is powerful. Jesus said not even the gates of hell can stop it. In fact, when the Church is persecuted, it seems to multiply and grow, because people get more serious about their faith.

Group Exercise: Let's picture this for a moment. We need several volunteers. Two will play lost, spiritually blind sinners and will stand behind others who represent the gates of hell. Two more will stand in front of the wall, seeking to release the prisoners from hell and bring them into God's kingdom. *Your teacher will lead you in this exercise.*

To the Group: What happens if you try to release the prisoners in your own strength?

____

____

What happens if you read God's Word, seek the Lord in prayer and fasting, and are confident in what he did on the cross? ____

____

____

This is what the churches we lead are supposed to do. We're to break through and set people free. People come into the body of Christ through evangelism.

NOTE: For instance, in America, 80 percent of the churches are not growing. Nineteen percent are growing because Christians are leaving other churches and joining those churches. Only one percent of all American churches are growing by evangelism. The good news is that 96 percent of people will visit a local church if invited.

* * *

Perhaps the most important thing you will teach your Timothys is how to share Jesus Christ with others. Every member of the local church must learn to share their faith. You are not called to do all the evangelism in the church, but you are called to teach members how to evangelize.

> Ephesians 4: 11-13 Now these are the gifts Christ gave to the church: the apostles, the prophets, the evangelists, and the pastors and teachers. Their responsibility is to equip God's people to do his work and build up the church, the body of Christ. This will continue until we all come to such unity in our faith and knowledge of God's Son that we will be mature in the Lord, measuring up to the full and complete standard of Christ.

Friendship and events are the two most common methods that attract people to Christ. We'll talk about events later. First, let's talk about the major way people come to faith—through personal relationships with believers.

Friendship Evangelism

To be effective in leading another human being to faith in the Lord Jesus Christ, you must have pure motives. Ask yourself, "Am I really befriending this person and treating them with love and respect, or are they just a number to me. Am I treating them nice because I want to say I led another person to Christ, or do I really care about them?"

If you really care about them, then God can use you, but you must be intentional. This is not hard to do, nor is it forcing the Gospel on people. The Holy Spirit will lead. You and I are simply tools that God has chosen to deliver his Good News, but first we must earn the right to do so.

Earlier in this book, I introduced the three-step **ADOPT 7** method for sharing Christ with an unbeliever. With ADOPT 7, you think of seven people you meet on a regular basis who are not Christians. Write their names down and begin to 1) Pray for them. 2) Serve them. 3) Share Jesus with them.

1. Pray for them. Every day, pray for the seven. Each time you see one of your ADOPT 7, pray for them to come to Christ.

2. Serve them. Go out of your way to get to know each one on your ADOPT 7 list. When you see them, stop, shake their hands, and help them with whatever they are doing. Look for any need they might have and try to fill it. Invite them to your home for a meal. Eventually, you will become their friend. This may take a while, perhaps years in some cases, but do not give up.

3. Share Jesus. As you love and serve them, they will eventually become your friends and will begin to ask why you are so different. Share with them what Jesus did for you. Present your testimony in three parts: What your life was like before meeting Jesus. How Jesus found you. How Jesus has changed your life.

Then ask them, "Could I share with you how Jesus could change your life?" If they say yes, you will have the opportunity to share the Gospel with them. If they choose to become a new Christian and part of God's family, then encourage them to also ADOPT 7 and introduce more people to Jesus.

Evangelism is loving people like Jesus loved people, and earning the right through friendship to give them the Gospel message. People will be attracted to Christ as they see you practicing what you preach. In the end, it is the Holy Spirit's job to convict them and bring them into a saving relationship with Jesus Christ. Your job is simply to pray, to serve, and to share.

Will you ADOPT 7?

Group Exercise: Fill in the blanks of this ADOPT 7 logo with the names of seven people you will pray for, serve, and share with, as you lead your congregation in friendship evangelism.

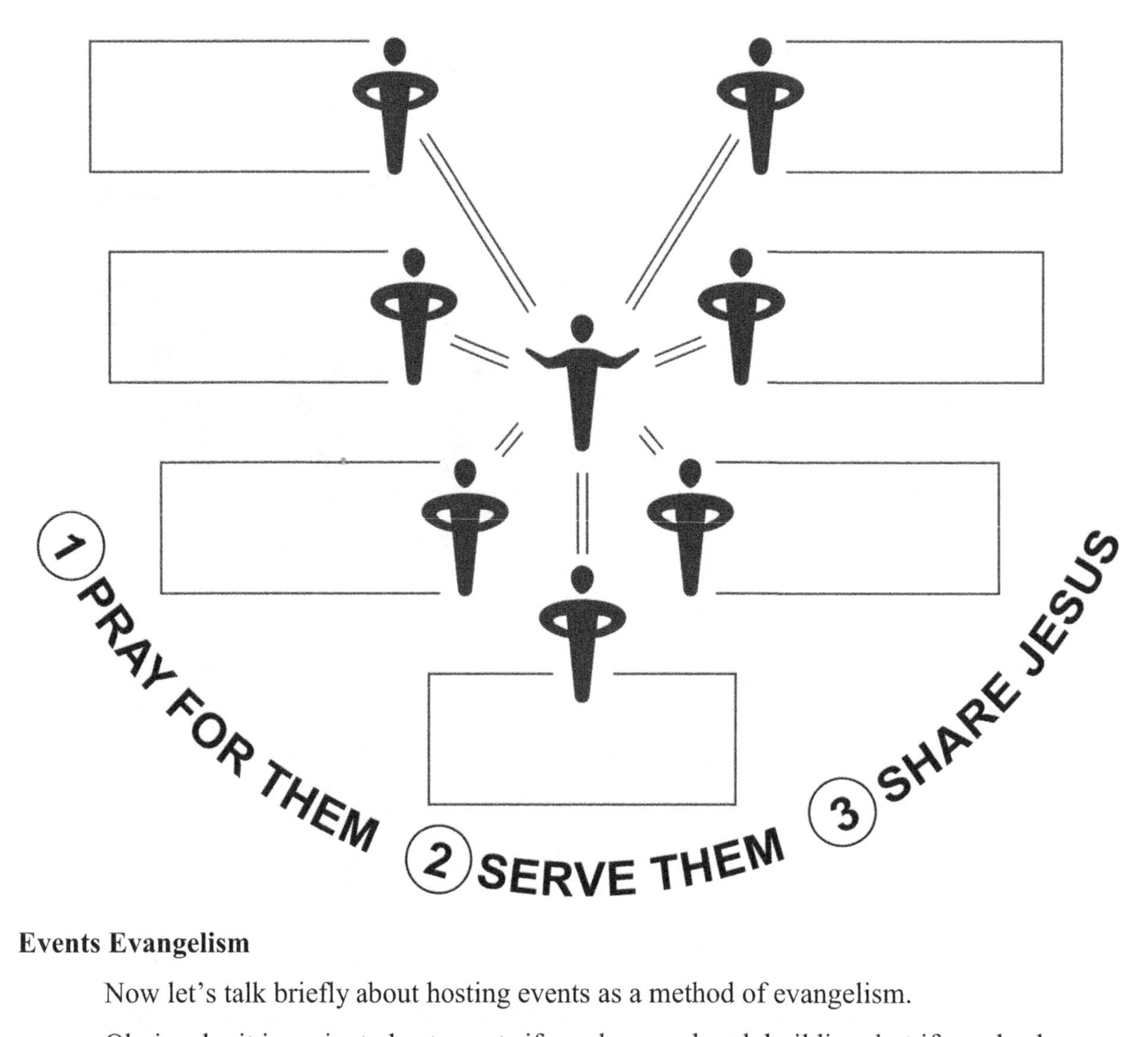

Events Evangelism

Now let's talk briefly about hosting events as a method of evangelism.

Obviously, it is easier to host events if you have a church building, but if you lead a house church you can still host events. Some of the most effective *event evangelism* may happen outside the place where you physically worship.

Event evangelism refers to inviting non-believing friends to special occasions, expecting they will meet other Christians. At these events, you will have an opportunity to hear their stories and share your own stories. Perhaps they'll hear a Gospel message, although not every event needs to include a formal Gospel presentation.

At our church, we have a big Christmas celebration to which we invite the surrounding community. We have programs for the children and for the adults. We have great food. We build friendships and share the gospel. The same thing is true at Easter.

Valentine's Day is another opportunity to invite people for good food, special music, fun, and some great fellowship. Perhaps you give a talk about love and very gently speak about the love of God. Invite people back the following weekend.

There will be many opportunities for members of your congregation to host events and invite their friends to come. Serve special food or feature cultural dances and songs. You don't have to get up and preach at every event. Simply show those attending that you are kind and caring and that the church is a loving place to be.

Another way to connect with people is to sponsor an activity that gives them the opportunity to help the poorest of the poor—like feeding the hungry, tutoring disadvantaged children, or fixing broken-down houses or cars. Find out what your community needs, form a team to address those needs, and invite your neighbors to join in. After these events, you could meet back at the church for a meal and a worship service.

One more example of event evangelism is the selection of a sermon topic interesting to the general population, like "How to Raise Respectful Children" or "How to Make Your Marriage Even Better." Invite everyone to come to this event and base your advice on the Bible. In the process, you'll acquaint your neighbors with what Christianity teaches. If they find your advice helpful, they'll be even more curious about who Jesus is and what he offers.

Group Exercise: List three events the church you pastor could host.

1. ____

   ____

2. ____

   ____

3. ____

   ____

Think about all the ways you can share Jesus and his values through events hosted by the church, but above all make sure that you and your Timothys are practicing evangelism.

Assimilation as a System

We'll define this system as *engaging lost people for Christ*. This is accomplished by inviting them to be part of a church community and getting them connected to the body.

An effective assimilation team will require a leader who loves people and is able to instruct and inspire others who love people. Strategize and have your team members ready to greet all visitors when they attend.

The more you connect with and engage first-time visitors, the more likely they are to become part of God's church. But you can't force it. Your welcome has to be genuine.

Assign specific people on the assimilation team to learn the names of those who visit the church and to let them know you're glad they came. Always smile. If appropriate, a team member should visit each first-timer in their homes, tell them about the church, and invite them back the following Sunday.

Notice each person's style and needs. Some don't want a lot of attention. That's okay. Others are lonely or searching. Know the difference.

If a local church hosts a children's event, learn the names of the parents as they drop their children off. By doing so, you can invite the children back to church for worship and encourage their parents to come as well. *NOTE: If visitors find something in a church for their children or young people, they're more likely to come back.*

When they come again, greet new people by name and ask others in the congregation to get to know them. Make it a mind-set that no one ever leaves a gathering without experiencing the warmth of God's love. Your attention and affection must be genuine, however. People can sense whether your love is real.

An effective assimilation team is important, but it is not all that is needed. You must be intentional about teaching the entire congregation how to be friendly towards others. Church members should always be looking for new faces and seeking to form new relationships.

The most important thing to remember is that we need to treat each visitor as special. Most of us, when we eat at a restaurant, decide to go back because of the quality of the food and how we were treated. The food could be exceptional, but if the service is not, we're probably not coming back. The same is true with the church.

We are God's children, the waiters, waitresses and cooks in his restaurant. People are spiritually hungry, and they've been going to the wrong places to eat. Jesus says he is the food we need. He is the living water that will cause them never to be thirsty again. What shows the way (or stands in the path) of a spiritually hungry person who wants to eat at his table is the warmth of his staff—you and me.

Worship as a System

Paul defines worship in his letter to the Romans.

> Romans 12:1-2 And so, dear brothers and sisters, I plead with you to give your bodies to God because of all he has done for you. Let them be a living and holy sacrifice—the kind he will find acceptable. This is truly the way to worship him. Don't copy the behavior and customs of this world, but let God transform you into a new person by changing the way you think. Then you will learn to know God's will for you, which is good and pleasing and perfect.

Above, Paul defines true worship as presenting ourselves to God daily, as living sacrifices. In Chapter 2, we discussed the need for each of us to live a *Life of Surrender.*

Before rising each morning, lie face down and visualize your bed or sleeping mat as an altar. Present yourself to God as a living sacrifice. Offer to him your thinking, your feelings, your will, and your physical body, as well as all your possessions and relationships.

This form of worship is personal.

When we come together, we engage in other forms of worship. They include the *Ministries of Testimony, Music, Giving and Communion*. These are all important, and we will address each at a later date.

However, one thing that will no longer be necessary in heaven is the *Ministry of the Message*. There will be no more preaching and no more sermons because we will all be saved. Until then, however, preaching is the primary way the Gospel of Jesus Christ is introduced to people's hearts and lives.

The Ministry of the Message

Is your preaching good? A lot of preaching and teaching is boring. People yawn and daydream. They count the flies on the ceiling or constantly check the time on their watches or cell phones, hoping you will finish. The *Ministry of the Message* should not be that way. It should be exciting, but not the kind of exciting where you yell at people. Preaching should tell them a story. If you want to experience God's power at work, preach his Word with power.

First, pray and ask God for direction. Then, think about the needs of your congregation. God's Spirit will guide you in planning what and how you are going to preach for the next several months.

Consider the steps involved in serving a meal. First, you plan what you will serve. Next, you buy the right ingredients. Finally, you prepare and serve the meal. Preaching is like planning and preparing a meal for your congregation. What foods do they need and in what form will they be most readily and gratefully consumed?

The easiest way to preach is to cover a book of the Bible like the Book of Mark or Paul's letter to the Philippians. Or, you may decide to choose a topic like fear, or the fruits of the Spirit, or the sovereignty of God, or how to share your faith.

Whatever you preach, it must be based on and supported by God's Word. I'm not going to focus on what you should preach. That's between you and God. But I will show you how to present your sermon or any Bible study or talk you may give.

The Itch and the Scratch[7]

Consider this way to make your message more interesting: find an *itch* and *scratch* it.

When a place on your body itches, you want to scratch it, right? Have you ever had an itch that you couldn't quite reach to scratch? It feels so good when someone comes along and scratches it for you, doesn't it? The same is true of a sermon which contains both an itch and a scratch. The itch is when you bring up a problem with which your listeners wrestle. The scratch is when you promise and then deliver the solution. Every sermon should present a problem (that's the itch) that causes people to want to know the solution (that's the scratch).

---

[7] Wilson, *Four Pages of Sermon*.

The Bible deals with our problems. Every passage of Scripture addresses some kind of problem and provides a solution.

When you plan your sermon, Bible study or talk, look at the Bible story you are preparing to tell. Ask yourself, "What is the itch (problem), and how does God scratch that itch (the solution he offers)?"

Group Exercise: Let's practice finding the itch and the scratch in the story of David and Goliath. *Your teacher will guide you in a role-play of 1 Samuel 17.*

To the Group: What is the itch? ____

What is the scratch? ____

If you preach David and Goliath and the itch is fear, you might begin by saying, "Everybody has giants in their lives. These giants may be sickness, death, poverty, what will happen to their children, loneliness, or many other fears."

Elaborate on some common fears, and people will start to itch as you speak. They will want to scratch and will lean in to listen. They'll wonder, "When is he going to give me a solution to my fears?"

Next, read all or parts of 1 Samuel 17. Talk about Goliath and how much Saul and the Israelites feared him. Point out that Goliath was their giant. Ask the congregation, "What are your giants?"

Call attention to the fact that David stepped onto the battlefield thinking the victory had already been won because his courageous faith in the greatness of God was bigger than Goliath. State your belief that whatever giants we face, we must trust in God and let him slay those giants.

"Like David," you can add, "our faithfulness will become a testimony to everyone who watches our lives, and they will give glory to God."

Preach like that, and people will listen.

HERE'S A TIP: Get your congregation to start itching and wanting the scratch early by bringing up the problem right at the beginning of your sermon.

A Drawback to Worship

Space is one limitation to worship in the local church. When your space gets too small, people will stop coming because it's too much of an effort—especially for someone who is not a Christian. They may already feel very uncomfortable and guilty, and may be looking for an excuse to stay home.

As a leader, you have to think of creative solutions.

For instance, you may have to consider having two services at two different times, if you stay in the same place. You may have to get a bigger place to accommodate your growing congregation.

Think creatively, and the Spirit of God will direct your paths.

Discipleship as a System[8]

Another system of the church which you must make sure is healthy and working is discipleship. This is the system by which the new believer is taught to follow Jesus and to introduce others to Jesus. The Book of Matthew offers us a definition of discipleship:

> Matthew 4:19 Jesus called out to them, "Come, follow me, and I will show you how to fish for people!"

From the scripture verse above, we learn that a disciple is one who actively follows Jesus, is being changed by Jesus, and is on mission with Jesus.

Discipleship is on-going, a learning process that never ends. Conversion is simply the first step, the beginning of a journey.

Under this definition of discipleship, we must shift from simply making converts to reaching people and discipling them. Paul, in his letter to the church in Colossae, spells out what discipleship in our churches should look like.

[8] Some of these discipleship concepts originated from Putman, Willis, Guindon and Krause, *Real-Life Discipleship Training Manual.*

> Colossians 1:28 So we tell others about Christ, warning everyone and teaching everyone with all the wisdom God has given us. We want to present them to God, perfect in their relationship to Christ.

Our goal should be to present people as mature in Christ. Making this the church's goal changes everything.

What does it mean to actively follow Jesus, to be changed by Jesus, and to be on mission with Jesus?

Actively Following Jesus

> John 12:26 "Anyone who wants to serve me must follow me, because my servants must be where I am. And the Father will honor anyone who serves me."

Jesus first said these words to Peter and Andrew when they were casting a net into the Sea of Galilee; these words were an invitation to follow Jesus.

In the discipleship process, Jesus is the leader. In order to be one of his disciples, we must accept his invitation to follow him. Accepting Jesus' invitation to follow him means to believe his Gospel. This is the first step in becoming a disciple of Jesus.

Going Deeper—Following Jesus first is a *head-level change*. Disciples need to understand who Jesus is: Master, Lord, Authority, Truth, Savior and Leader. They must acknowledge him as such by confessing belief in him. Finally, they must make a commitment to follow him and be in relationship with him.

Making a decision to follow Jesus in turn affects how a disciple thinks. This head-level change challenges everything from our worldview to our priorities. Peter, James and John believed that Jesus was the Messiah. They were so convinced that they took a drastic step.

> Matthew 4:20 And they left their nets at once and followed him.

Being a disciple of Jesus and discipling others is not always easy; in fact, Jesus promised his followers would face difficulty.

> John 16:33b "Here on earth you will have many trials and sorrows. But take heart, because I have overcome the world."

Group Exercise: Examine the following passage from the Book of Luke and discuss what Jesus requires from his disciples.

> Luke 9:23-24 Then he said to the crowd, "If any of you wants to be my follower, you must give up your own way, take up your cross daily, and follow me. If you try to hang on to your life, you will lose it. But if you give up your life for my sake, you will save it."

Think back to when Jesus called you to be his disciple. Was there anything preventing you from making that decision? Did Jesus call you to leave something behind or to pick something up?

____

____

____

____

Now, think about the group you lead or hope to lead. Perhaps not all of your members are yet disciples of Jesus. What could be some possible hindrances for these members?

____

____

____

____

A REMINDER: Following Jesus does not always mean we need to leave our homes and loved ones in order to follow Him—although some will make this sacrifice. Often, what many of us need to leave behind is our self, namely our selfish desires and ambitions.

Being Changed by Jesus

Jim Putman suggests that becoming a disciple involves more than just a one-time choice. "Not only must we make a mental decision to follow Christ; there must also be a process of transformation in which a work takes place in our heart and affections."[9]

This second aspect of discipleship focuses on the change Jesus wants to make in each of his followers. Paul reveals that change in the first of his letters to the churches.

> Romans 8:29 For God knew his people in advance, and he chose them to become like his Son, so that his Son would be the firstborn among many brothers and sisters.

God transforms disciples of Jesus to be more and more like his Son—to make their hearts more like the heart of Jesus.

We cannot mistakenly assume people have to change themselves before being able to follow Jesus. Jesus calls people before any change occurs in them. Disciples of Jesus are not chosen because of who they already are. Jesus chooses them because he knows who they can become. In following Jesus, disciples need to be willing to be unmade in order to be remade in his image and likeness.

The second aspect of discipleship involves *heart-level change*. Jesus changes his disciples into new people including their character, attributes and priorities.

It is important to recognize that God is ultimately the one bringing about the changes. In particular, the Holy Spirit who lives within all disciples of Jesus is responsible for their transformation.

As a result of this transformation, certain characteristics will be produced in the lives of Jesus' disciples. These characteristics are named in Paul's letter to the Galatians.

> Galatians 5:22-23 But the Holy Spirit produces this kind of fruit in our lives: love, joy, peace, patience, kindness, goodness, faithfulness, gentleness, and self-control. There is no law against these things!

The Book of John also reveals that God will cut off those who bear no fruit, but will continue to *prune* those who do bear fruit so they will be even more fruitful.

---

[9] Putman, Harrington, *DiscipleShift*, Page 48.

> John 15:1-2 "I am the true grapevine, and my Father is the gardener. He cuts off every branch of mine that doesn't produce fruit, and he prunes the branches that do bear fruit so they will produce even more."

The Nature of Change. Change does not always happen instantaneously. God changes disciples of Jesus over time and through a relationship with his Son—this is the key ingredient.

The supernatural changes that Jesus brings about in his disciples should then be evidenced by their love for God and their love for others.

Group Exercise: How have you changed since you became a follower of Jesus? ____________

____

____

____

In light of our goal to make more disciples of Jesus Christ and present them as mature in Christ, what are some activities or methods we could encourage each other to do so as to allow the Holy Spirit to transform and grow us? ____

____

____

____

Committed to the Mission of Jesus

When Jesus called his first disciples, he used language these fishermen would understand. However, instead of fishing for fish they were to fish for people. Fishers of men seek to make disciples of all nations; they are committed to the mission Jesus gave them.

As Jim Putman puts it, "The people we know and love who do not know Jesus are lost for eternity unless they accept Christ as their Lord and Savior. When we believe this reality, it changes the way we think, pray, and spend our time and money. We understand that there are only two categories of people: the saved and the unsaved."[10]

---

[10] Putman, Willis, Guindon and Krause, *Real-Life Discipleship Training Manual,* 31.

Discipleship is an active process. It cannot be limited to simply sitting and listening. This third aspect of discipleship involves a *hands-on change*, and disciples of Jesus are to be actively committed to Jesus' mission.

"The beauty of God's plan is that we do not do the work of discipleship alone," says Putman.[11] The discipleship process goes both ways. There are people helping us as we help others.

Group Exercise: What are some ways you have actively followed through on Jesus' mission to make disciples? ____________________

____

____

____

Leading a small group is certainly one way to be actively committed to Jesus' mission. We need to encourage those we are discipling to be committed to that mission as well. List ways people in your group could apply the mission of Jesus in their own lives.

____

____

____

Caring as a System

As a pastor, we must care for the people God has put under us. This is most effectively done through small groups of 7-12 people who meet together regularly and who are also part of the larger congregation. One of the functions of these small groups is to encourage believers to study the Word of God and grow in their faith.

The pastor initiates this by:

- Preparing a sermon for the weekend.

[11] ibid., 37.

- Writing questions about the sermon for small groups to answer when they meet the following week.
- Providing other Scriptures to help these groups go deeper into the Word of God.

The small group leaders direct these discussions, which make use of the gifts of teaching within the group.

* * *

Whether practiced in a small group or individually, there is a method of Bible study you can teach your people that encourages each person to feed themselves rather than depending entirely on you or the small group leader to teach the Word of God.

In English, you may remember this method of Bible study by the letters S.O.A.P.[12]

Scripture – Read a chapter of the Bible every day. Out of that chapter, ask God to impress on you one (or at the most two) verses of Scripture to study in greater depth.

Observation – Make an observation about the verse(s). In other words, answer the question, "What is this verse saying to me?"

Application – Write down how the verse(s) of Scripture applies to your life.

Prayer – Take everything you've learned from the verse(s) and turn it into a prayer to God.

Group Exercise: Let's practice this method of Bible study together by reading Psalm 1.

To the Group: What did you learn from this exercise?

____

____

____

____

[12] Adapted from Wayne Cordeiro. "What's SOAP?" https://discoveronething.files.wordpress.com/2015/01/soap.pdf

* * *

Another function of small groups is to provide care for the individual members of each small group.

Every small group should have a leader who acts as its shepherd—someone who also has the gift of mercy or of counseling. The leader's job is to look after the people in the group. If someone is in financial need, the shepherd should rally the group to help. If someone is depressed or despondent, the shepherd should provide counseling or seek the assistance of someone with that gift. If someone is sick, the shepherd must pray with them and keep the pastor informed. In these ways, the shepherd assists the pastor.

If the person is very sick, in need, or despondent, and the congregation is small enough, the pastor must also visit them. But the pastor should make sure the person requiring attention understands that the leader of the small group, the shepherd, has the greatest responsibility for providing care.

The larger the congregation, the harder it will be for the pastor to care for each believer personally. See Acts 6 where the early church found this to be true and appointed seven people "full of the Spirit and wisdom" to provide that necessary care. When the present-day church grows beyond 75 people, the pastor cannot lead the congregation and move it forward while, at the same time, caring for individual needs.

This is a difficult truth to accept, but it is critical that we take it seriously if the local church is to continue growing. The Bible refers to all of us as priests and ministers. Like the apostles did in managing the growth of the early church, the pastor must empower others to represent the Lord in caring for the individual needs of the congregation. As stated earlier, all church members must be considered prospective Timothys. Some will stay to help the pastor grow the existing church, and some will go out to plant new churches.

PLEASE NOTE: When you choose men and women who will help you by providing care, do this in front of the entire congregation. Pray over them publicly so the entire church knows that you have trained them and that they represent you.

Stewardship as a System

Everything belongs to God, no matter how much or how little you have. The shirt you wear belongs to God. Your body belongs to God. Your house belongs to God. God tells us so in the Book of Genesis.

In the beginning, God planted a garden with many fruit trees. He also created a man and a woman. He put them in his garden to care for it. By this action, he proclaimed Adam and Eve stewards or managers of his property.

"You are free to eat from any tree in the garden," God told Adam, "but you may not eat from the tree of the knowledge of good and evil, for when you eat from it you will certainly die."[13]

When God created Adam and Eve, they thought only of God and of each other. They did not think about themselves. As a result, they were not aware of being naked. They had nothing to hide.

But Satan disguised himself as a serpent and approached Eve. He urged her to eat from the forbidden tree. Apparently, Adam had passed God's Word to Eve because she told the serpent that would result in death.

"You will not certainly die," said the serpent to the woman. "For God knows that when you eat from it your eyes will be opened, and you will be like God, knowing good and evil."[14] Satan implied that Eve would not need God anymore if she ate from the tree.

Eve decided to take what did not belong to her, and she ate it. She gave some fruit from the forbidden tree to Adam, who should have known better since God spoke to him originally about the tree. But he ate the fruit, too.

Immediately, self-awareness and selfishness entered God's perfect world. Both Adam and Eve knew what they had done was wrong. They ran away, hid, and covered themselves with fig leaves because of their fear and shame. Their greatest guilt came from knowing they had taken what did not belong to them.

Starting in Genesis, the Bible makes clear that everything belongs to God. All God asks is that we give him back a small piece of what we've been given to manage, to remind us of his ownership. He introduced tithing in Genesis 14 and the root word is mentioned 29 times in the New International Version® of the Old Testament. Tithing and stewardship go hand-in-hand.

---

[13] Genesis 2:16-17 (NIV®)
[14] Genesis 3:4-5 (NIV®)

Some say God no longer requires us to tithe; but, in fact, Jesus reaffirms the tithe in the New Testament Book of Matthew.

All the rest is ours to manage. Yet, just as Eve focused her attention on the forbidden tree, we focus our attention on that small piece that God asks from us. We think it is ours, and we want it back.

No matter how poor, you have something to give God that is rightfully his. You might not be wealthy, but if you raise chickens, goats, or a have a garden, you should sell the eggs, milk, and produce, and give God his tithe before using the rest. Teach this to your Timothy and instruct him to teach his people at least once a year about good stewardship.

But listen carefully. As pastors, we must set the example. We must tithe or we are stealing from God, as Eve and Adam did. Make sure you practice good stewardship before teaching others, or God will deal with your heart.

Below is a creative way to teach stewardship.

Group Exercise: Take a cake and cut it into ten pieces. Put one piece on a plate and hold the rest of the cake in your other hand. Say, "Imagine the single piece represents God's share (one-tenth) and the rest of the cake represents everything you own…" *Your teacher will show you what else to say.*

To the Group: What did you learn from this exercise? ____

____

____

____

____

____

Leadership as a System

Leadership as a system describes the process you create for selecting and training your leaders and church planters. As I emphasized at the beginning of Chapter 2, leadership rises and falls on character. As you recruit and train your leaders, consider what leadership expert John Maxwell describes as *The 21 Indispensable Qualities of a Leader*, reprinted below.

These qualities are not automatic. You must be intentional in training and mentoring your students to become the leaders they are capable of being.

The 21 Indispensable Qualities of a Leader[15]

1. Character: Be a Piece of the Rock

- Character Is More Than Talk
- Talent Is a Gift, but Character is a Choice
- Character Brings Lasting Success with People
- Leaders Cannot Rise Above the Limitations [Level] of Their Character

2. Charisma: The First Impression Can Seal the Deal

- Love Life
- Put a "10" on Every Person's Head
- Give People Hope
- Share Yourself

3. Commitment: It Separates Doers from Dreamers

- Commitment Starts in the Heart
- Commitment Is Tested by Action
- Commitment Opens the Door to Achievement

4. Communication: Without It, You Travel Alone

- Simplify Your Message
- See the Person
- Show the Truth
- Seek a Response

5. Competence: If You Build It, They Will Come

- Show Up Every Day
- Keep Improving
- Follow Through with Excellence
- Accomplish More than Expected

---

[15] Maxwell, *21 Indispensable Qualities Leader.*

- Inspire Others

6. Courage: One Person with Courage Is a Majority

- Courage Begins with an Inward Battle
- Courage is Making Things Right, Not Just Smoothing Them Over
- Courage in a Leader Inspires Commitment from Followers
- Your Life Expands in Proportion to Your Courage

7. Discernment: Put an End to Unsolved Mysteries

- Discover the Root Issues
- Enhance Your Problem Solving
- Evaluate Your Options for Maximum Impact
- Multiply Your Opportunities

8. Focus: The Sharper It Is, The Sharper You Are

- Focus 70 Percent on Strengths
- Focus 25 Percent on New Things
- Focus 5 Percent on Weaknesses [Delegate]
- [Shift to Your Strengths and Staff Your Weaknesses]

9. Generosity: Your Candle Loses Nothing When It Lights Another

- Be Grateful for Whatever You Have
- Put People First
- Don't Allow the Desire for Possessions to Control You
- Regard Money as a Resource
- Develop a Habit of Giving

10. Initiative: You Won't Leave Home Without It

- [Leaders] Know What They Want
- [Leaders] Push Themselves to Act
- [Leaders] Take More Risks
- [Leaders] Make More Mistakes

11. Listening: To Connect with Their Hearts, Use Your Ears

- [Listen to] Your Followers
- [Listen to] Your Customers
- [Listen to] Your Competitors
- [Listen to] Your Mentors

12. Passion: Take This Life and Love It

- Passion Is the First Step to Achievement
- Passion Increases Your Willpower
- Passion Changes You
- Passion Makes the Impossible Possible

13. Positive Attitude: If You Believe You Can, You Can
- Your Attitude Is a Choice
- Your Attitude Determines Your Actions
- Your People Are a Mirror of Your Attitude
- Maintaining a Good Attitude Is Easier Then Regaining One

14. Problem Solving: You Can't Let Your Problems Be a Problem
- [Leaders] Anticipate Problems
- [Leaders] Accept the Truth
- [Leaders] See the Big Picture
- [Leaders] Handle One Thing at a Time
- [Leaders] Don't Give Up a Major Goal When [In the Valleys]

15. Relationships: If You Get Along, They'll Go Along
- Have a Leaders Head - Understand People
- Have a Leaders Heart - Love People
- Extend a Leaders Hand - Help People

16. Responsibility: If You Won't Carry the Ball, You Can't Lead the Team
- [Leaders] Get the Job Done
- [Leaders] Go the Extra Mile
- [Leaders] Be Driven By Excellence
- [Leaders] Produce, Regardless of the Situation

17. Security: Competence Never Compensates for Insecurity
- [Insecure Leaders] Don't Provide Security for Others
- [Insecure Leaders] Take More from People than They Give
- [Insecure Leaders] Continually Limit Their Best People
- [Insecure Leaders] Continually Limit the Organization

18. Self-Discipline: The First Person You Lead Is Yourself
- Develop and Follow Your Priorities
- Make a Disciplined Lifestyle Your Goal
- Challenge Your Excuses
- [Delay] Rewards Until the Job Is Done
- Stay Focused on Results

19. Servanthood: To Get Ahead, Put Others First
- [A True Servant Leader] Puts Others Ahead of His Own Agenda
- [A True Servant Leader] Possesses the Confidence to Serve
- [A True Servant Leader] Initiates Service to Others
- [A True Servant Leader] Is Not "Position-Conscious
- [A True Servant Leader] Serves Out of Love

20. Teachability: To Keep Leading, Keep Learning

- Cure Your "Destination Disease" [Arriving But Not Growing]
- Overcome Your Success
- Swear Off Shortcuts
- Trade in Your Pride
- Never Pay Twice for the Same Mistake

21. Vision: You Can Seize Only What You Can See

- Vision Starts Within
- Vision Draws on Your History
- Vision Meets Others' Needs
- Vision Helps You Gather Resources

If you wish to study these qualities in greater depth, you may purchase Maxwell's book on Amazon.com. In my next book, I will discuss the keys of leadership implementation.

When Systems Break Down

You may ask, "Does the pastor serve in a particular system?" Yes, the pastor is always part of the **worship system**, because he's the primary teacher and communicator. I say primary—but not the only one. In some churches, there might be a team of preachers. But the pastor is the lead teacher and the primary voice.

Also, all pastors have strengths, and they will always move towards the system that can best use these strengths. If they like counseling, then they'll pay more attention to **Care as a System**. If they like training, then they'll gravitate toward **Leadership as a System.**

Ultimately, it is the pastor's responsibility to make sure that all the systems of the church have passionate leaders overseeing them.

Wherever a system is strong, be thankful and make sure it stays strong.

Wherever a system is weak or broken down, it's your responsibility to fix it. But be careful. If you have four weak systems, don't make the mistake of trying to change them all at once. You won't have the time or energy. It can be overwhelming to you and confusing to your congregation.

Choose one weak system and put all your energy into making it stronger. When it's strong, choose another. Focus on improving one system at a time.

* * *

If your physical body becomes ill, you go to a doctor who will try to determine which system is not working right. He'll give you medicine or perform surgery to help heal that sickness. This is important because, if one system isn't working right, it can affect your whole body.

The same is true of the local church. All systems must be healthy and working the way God intended or it can affect the whole body of Christ.

If there's trouble in the church, aside from sin, there is usually something wrong with one or more of the systems. As a leader, it's your job to figure out which one isn't working properly and to know how to fix it.

The purpose of this entire guide is to help you lead a healthy, growing church. Your constant and prayerful attention to the systems of the local church will enable you to carry out the ministry of Christ in a world which desperately needs Him.

CHAPTER 7
Concluding Remarks

Having met and spoken, on behalf of TTI, with hundreds of Pauls and Timothys, I am greatly encouraged. Your bravery and faith will sustain and enable you to take the hope of the Gospel to your own region, resulting in life transformation.

My parents, James and Virginia Hummel, were the very first missionaries to the western highlands of Papua New Guinea. They went on little more than raw faith and courage, with the conviction that God wanted to transform the lives of an ancient people.

Much like the early apostles, my father met with the natives and formed relationships as he sought to understand their culture and find ways to communicate the Gospel. Soon, he saw a handful of converts and began to pour himself into those new believers, helping them understand who Jesus was, what the Bible says, and how to disciple others—from evangelism to pastoral care.

From that handful of men and women grew a church of over 10,000 people, based on many of the principles you've studied in *How to Lead the Church.*

My father never had to be in control. He was a leader, but he gave authority to the men and women under him, and the Gospel spread like wildfire. Though they came from a Stone Age culture, these believers were truly apostles. As a young boy, I saw the model of disciples making disciples work in the most primitive of places.

The principles taught in this book have been tried and proven, from the days of Jesus to these modern times. I am convinced that as each Paul and Timothy puts these principles into practice, God will be faithful, fruit will be produced, and hearts and lives will be changed.

May God richly bless you. – *Pastor Hummel*

APPENDIX A
Another Leader Like Joseph

Is what was true in Joseph's life true for all good leaders? Consider the life of Daniel who originally lived in Jerusalem. In 586 BC, because of the sinfulness of his chosen people, God allowed King Nebuchadnezzar to invade Jerusalem and destroy it. Nebuchadnezzar took many of the Jews captive to Babylon. Daniel was one of them—along with his three friends: Shadrach, Meshach and Abednego.

The prophet Jeremiah had told the Jewish people they would be exiles for 70 years and told them how to face their captivity:

> Jeremiah 29: 4-7 This is what the LORD of Heaven's Armies, the God of Israel, says to all the captives he has exiled to Babylon from Jerusalem: "Build homes, and plan to stay. Plant gardens, and eat the food they produce. Marry and have children. Then find spouses for them so that you may have many grandchildren. Multiply! Do not dwindle away! And work for the peace and prosperity of the city where I sent you into exile. Pray to the LORD for it, for its welfare will determine your welfare."

How did Daniel and his friends act while they were captives in that foreign land? Did they turn their backs to the Babylonians and form a tight circle to keep out the sinful culture? Or did they look for opportunities to argue with the Babylonians, condemning them and fighting against them? They did none of these.

These words are very important for us today. God, who never changes, is telling us through these verses how we should live and teach our people to live in an unbelieving world. God tells us to live peacefully, making friendships with the communities that God has put us in—even if they eat different food, speak a different language, dress in different ways and have other customs that are different from ours. He tells us to work diligently, not just for our own success but for the success of people around us, and he tells us to pray for the prosperity of the people of the communities in which we live.

The first thing Daniel and his friends were faced with was choosing what part of the Babylonian culture they could accept and what they could not accept. They accepted new names, they wore different clothes, and they learned the Babylonian language.

But in Chapter 1 of the Book of Daniel, they refused to eat the meat and other kinds of food that God had forbidden his chosen people to eat. Daniel and his friends convinced their captors, instead, to feed them vegetables. As a result, they flourished. Like Joseph did, **Daniel and his friends always trusted in God's control**, and God honored that.

In Chapter 2 of the Book of Daniel, King Nebuchadnezzar had a troubling dream and the wise men closest to him could not interpret it. So he gave the order to kill all his wise men. When they heard this would happen, the young Jewish men fasted and prayed. God gave them the interpretation of the king's dream, so Nebuchadnezzar did not execute all the wise men. Instead, the king elevated Daniel and his friends to high offices in his kingdom. Like Joseph, **they always did their best.** Their best was to seek the Lord when all earthly solutions were exhausted. God honored that.

Finally, in Chapter 3, Shadrach, Meshach, and Abednego refused to worship a golden image made by King Nebuchadnezzar. As a result, they were thrown into a fiery furnace. "Even if we die, we're not going to bow down," said the three as they were put in the furnace. "If God wants to rescue us, he will. If he doesn't, that's okay." God honored that. Not one hair on their heads was burned and the king promoted them.

Chapter 6 reveals a similar situation that threatened Daniel's life. He was thrown into a lion's den for refusing to pray to the king. God honored that by closing the lions' mouths. As a result, Daniel prospered in his service to the foreign king. Like Joseph did, **Daniel and his friends always remained faithful to God, no matter what happened.**

* * *

Besides the characteristics we have observed in the lives of both Joseph and Daniel, we can identify three more principles of leadership.

1. **Power and position did not corrupt them.** They served God, not man and not themselves. If you want God to use you as a leader—if you want to see a spiritual revival in your country—do not yield to the temptation to please men or please

yourself. Don't try to please your congregation or your denominational leaders. Stay focused on God. Please Him.

2. **They always gave God the glory.** Daniel never took credit for himself. Neither did Joseph. They always gave credit to God. As a result, God lifted them to high positions. In my culture—and maybe in yours—people try to rise up by talking about how great they are and about all their accomplishments. But in God's economy, when we give him the credit, he raises us up.
3. **Their power came from a life of prayer and fasting.** Joseph, as well as Daniel and his friends, spent a lot of time seeking God. As a result, God worked through them. This is a huge problem in the church today. We don't want to pray. We don't want to fast. We want to act right away. These Old Testament stories teach us that it is more important to seek God's will and let him empower us to accomplish his glory.

APPENDIX B

Three Things Volunteer Leaders Must Know

Most of the leaders in our churches are volunteers. That's probably something you don't think about as you work together toward a common mission and vision. Volunteers are not paid, but to do their best, they need something from you. They must know:

1. **That you love and care for them** and their families.
2. **That they are helping you make a difference** in the work of the church.
3. **How they can improve.**

Love and Care – Get to know their names and learn about their families. Ask about their jobs and what else they do. Learn about their struggles as well as what makes them happy. People want to be known. They want to sense that you care deeply for them. If you don't feel that, they will feel used and they won't be loyal to you.

Jesus took a lot of time to get to know his disciples. Everywhere they went, they would walk and talk together. What we have in the Bible is only a small part of all the time they spent with Him. The Book of John says, "If everything Jesus did and said was written down there are not enough books in the world to contain it."

The leaders you are training, your Timothys, need to know **that you love and care for them**, which means you must intentionally spend time with them.

Making a Difference – People like to know the value of their efforts in other people's lives. As they grow in their roles and take responsibility for the tasks you have given them, write your leaders emails or notes. Take them out for coffee or tea. Let them know you see how God is using them and **that they are helping make a difference** in the work of the church.

How to Improve – Finally, tell your leaders **how they can improve.** Give them small ways to get better and challenge them to follow through. When they do, be sure to point out their successes and compliment them.

Most pastors recruit volunteers, give them jobs, quickly tell them what they want them to do, and then leave them alone.

They try their best, but they seldom receive an encouraging word. All they ever hear is "You're not doing it right" or they hear nothing. They get discouraged and quit. Then the job comes back to the pastor. Do that too many times, and volunteers will begin saying *no*.

People will do more if you encourage them and reward them **for improving**, if they know they are **making a difference** and if they **know that you care**.

BIBLIOGRAPHY

Chapter 2

Hersey, Paul. *The Situational Leader*. New York: Warner Books, March 1985.

Meyers, Kevin and John Maxwell. *Home Run: Learn God's Game Plan for Life and Leadership*. New York: Faithworks, Hachette Book Group, 2014.

Chapter 4

Borden, Paul. *Hit the Bullseye: How Denominations Can Aim the Congregation at the Missions Field*. Nashville: Abington Press, 2003.

Chapter 5

Lencioni, Patrick. *The Three Signs of a Miserable Job: A Fable for Managers (and their employees)*. San Francisco: Jossey-Bass, a Wiley Imprint, 2007.

Chapter 6

Cordeiro, Wayne. "What's SOAP?" https://discoveronething.files.wordpress.com/2015/01/soap.pdf

Maxwell, John C. *The 21 Indispensable Qualities of a Leader*. Nashville: Thomas Nelson, 1999.

Putman, Jim, Avery T. Willis, Brandon Guindon, and Bill Krause. *Real-Life Discipleship Training Manual: Equipping Disciples Who Make Disciples*. Colorado Springs: NavPress, 2010.

Putman, Jim and Bob Harrington. *DiscipleShift*. Grand Rapids: Zondervan, 2013.

Wilson, Paul Scott. *The Four Pages of the Sermon, Revised and Updated*. Nashville: Abingdon Press, 2018.

NOTES

Made in the USA
Monee, IL
11 April 2021